I0794466

The View through your Window

Other Books by the Singletons

Setting Up Stones: Making Your Home a Place of Worship

Let It Shine! Partnering with God to Raise World Changers

With Annie and Robbie Bridges:

Schooled! Taming Your First Year of College

"Greg and Martha Singleton live a life of vision for family, faith, and future generations. *The View through Your Window* is both a testimony and a guide to gaining a future that works through the generations, especially for those whose heritage lacks these very things. With simple and profound truths and a lifetime of practice, the Singletons offer a gift to us all. Do you need a clear vision for your family? Then take their advice! Given with wisdom, depth, and humor, they offer to us all a proven recipe for deepening the foundations of faith, family, and the future."

—**Dennis Gallaher,** Senior Pastor, Freedom Fellowship, New Braunfels, TX

"Greg and Martha have not only written an inspirational book, but one that serves as a wise guide in developing a godly vision for you and your family. We live in a world that is constantly telling us what to love and live for, but in the end we only find ourselves with earthly treasures that do not last. *The View through Your Window* cuts through the cultural noise and provides the necessary tools to develop and live out your family's unique, God-inspired vision. I'm confident many lives will be impacted by this book!"

—**Ryan Gikas,** Pastor of Music & Arts, Bridgeway Church, Oklahoma City; cofounder, The Verses Project

"Greg and Martha Singleton get it. They understand that what ultimately matters as we raise our children is that we introduce them to God and point them toward his mission and purpose for their lives."

—**Bob Lepine,** cohost, *FamilyLife Today*

"Martha and Greg have made a strategic spiritual contribution to today's families by sharing practical, relevant, exciting ways to make our homes true places of worship—homes where our children can learn to love God, live for him, apply his Word effectively in their daily lives, as well as how to live out God's wonderful plan for their lives and impact others for him as they go."

—**Wanda Bailey,** Children's Ministry Coordinator, Billy Graham Evangelistic Association

"Martha and Greg Singleton will inspire parents to see their children as the world-changers that God created them to be, and to equip them to live the greatest adventure on earth—following Christ and his purpose for their lives."

—**Cheri Fuller**, author, speaker

"The Singletons do a good job of offering hope, and that hope will bring peace, comfort, and a host of other good stuff. Thank you for reminding me of the little things that matter."

—**Byron Weathersbee, EdD,** Vice President of Student Affairs, University of Mary Hardin Baylor; President, Legacy Family Ministries

"Thanks so much, Greg and Martha, for speaking to our MOPS groups! Your message will surely echo in our homes in the days that follow. Thank you so much for introducing the steps, and giving so many examples of 'how-to' come to a clear, godly vision for our homes and families."

—**Susan Berlin,** Mothers of Pre-Schoolers (MOPS) Coordinator, Houston

"I hope that God creates a viral movement that multiplies your ministry ten times. Nothing, absolutely nothing, would thrill me more!"

—**Dr. Dennis Rainey,** President, FamilyLife

The View through your Window

FINDING GOD'S VISION FOR YOUR FAMILY

MARTHA & GREG SINGLETON

LEAFWOOD
PUBLISHERS
an imprint of Abilene Christian University Press

THE VIEW THROUGH YOUR WINDOW

Finding God's Vision for Your Family

LEAFWOOD
PUBLISHERS
an imprint of Abilene Christian University Press

Copyright © 2017 by Martha & Greg Singleton

ISBN 978-0-89112-383-5

Printed in the United States of America

ALL RIGHTS RESERVED
No part of this publication may be reproduced, stored in a retrieval system, or transmitted in any form by any means—electronic, mechanical, photocopying, recording, or otherwise—without prior written consent.

Scripture quotations, unless otherwise noted, are from the Holy Bible, New Living Translation, copyright ©1996, 2004, 2007, 2015 by Tyndale House Foundation. Used by permission of Tyndale House Publishers, Inc., Carol Stream, IL 60188. All rights reserved.

Scripture quotations noted *The Message* taken from *The Message*. Copyright © 1993, 1994, 1995, 1996, 2000, 2001, 2002. Used by permission of NavPress Publishing Group.

Scripture quotations noted NIV are taken from The Holy Bible, New International Version®, NIV®. Copyright © 1973, 1978, 1984, 2011 by Biblica, Inc.® Used by permission. All rights reserved worldwide.

Scripture quotations noted TLB are taken from The Living Bible copyright © 1971 by Tyndale House Foundation. Used by permission of Tyndale House Publishers Inc., Carol Stream, IL 60188. All rights reserved.

Scripture quotations noted *The Voice* are taken from The Voice™. Copyright © 2008 by Ecclesia Bible Society. Used by permission. All rights reserved.

Scripture quotations noted KJV are taken from the King James Version of the Bible.

Published in association with the Hartline Literary Agency, 123 Queenston Drive, Pittsburgh, PA 15235.

Cover design by ThinkPen Design, LLC
Interior text design by Sandy Armstrong, Strong Design

Leafwood Publishers is an imprint of Abilene Christian University Press
ACU Box 29138
Abilene, Texas 79699

1-877-816-4455
www.leafwoodpublishers.com

17 18 19 20 21 22 / 7 6 5 4 3 2 1

Dedication

For the things we saw from day to day in our homes as we were growing up:

Acceptance, approval, kindness, forgiveness, grace, love, and faith, added to great meals and lots of laughter

Fathers who went out of their way to quietly, sometimes even secretly, share what little they had with others who had needs

Mothers who were open and friendly and nurturing, not only to us, but to our friends and any others who came through our doors

We dedicate this book to the memory of our parents, Jo and C. B. Singleton and Norma and Barney McMullan.

For the heritage of faith that has been kept and passed down to us through generations:

Ancestors whose families were people of integrity and service in their communities

Those who, in each generation and place that they settled, set aside part of their land and built churches

Who served as pastors and worship leaders and teachers and elders and deacons

Siblings and cousins who continue to serve and care for people today

We dedicate this book to the relatives, past and present, who keep and enlarge God's vision for our extended families.

For the example we saw in other families of faith over the years:

Places where we again could see acceptance, forgiveness, grace, and love

Integrity and service and caring for the needs of others

Along with the joy and the laughter and the fun of faithful friends

We dedicate this book to the Strongs, the Cains, the Roses, the Prices, the Carrolls, and the Sturdys.

For the fulfillment of seeing our children and grandchildren seek out and follow God's vision:

Choosing, from early childhood through adulthood, to contribute to an atmosphere of kindness, grace, love, and faith, added to time spent together and lots of laughter

Going out of your way to share what you have with those who have needs

Paying special attention to the overlooked and those without voices

Being open and friendly and nurturing to all who God brings across your path

We dedicate this book to Annie and Robbie, Josiah and Levi, and to Matt and Sarah, and to all of the precious Re:Church members added to our family.

And most of all, for revealing to us a vision for what our family could be:

Giving his Son for the forgiveness of our sins, unending mercy, and amazing grace

Faithfully providing all that we need, with blessings heaped up and running over

Ever true to his Word

We dedicate this book to the glory of God, in the lives and in the homes of every person who may come to read it!

Martha & Greg Singleton

Table of Contents

Part Three: Looking Out Your Window

Part Four: Making Vision Work

Part One

Clearing Your Vision

Chapter One

Were You Raised in a Barn?

We love it when a couple comes to us, glowing, announcing that they're going to have their first baby. We always smile back at them. They think we're smiling at them because we're happy for them and, of course, that's partially true. But our smiles are mainly because we know they have no idea about the wild ride they've signed up for!

When you become a parent, your perspective on almost everything changes. There are those obvious transitions that take place, like losing sleep, changing diapers, having another mouth to feed, and considering another little person in all your plans. Some of the things that happen, though, you just can't anticipate. These are the daily challenges of parenthood that are so outrageous, so foreign to your preparenting lifestyle, they take you completely by surprise. No matter how precious and perfect your kids might be, no parents are immune. When God blessed your home with kids, very often that neat little reality package you had put together in your head was completely shattered.

You can't really grasp the essence of what it might be like until you're right in the middle of the situation. But expect that during those moments, your entire routine—check that—your entire reality will be shaken at its foundations. Even if you had a thought that something as crazy as this might happen, you still could never have been braced for it. So here's a heads-up for you. In response to the outrageous, under the pressure of the moment, even your vocabulary will expand to include some amazing phrases. Here are two of our classics.

"Don't ever eat your cup!" (Said as our three-year-old, Matt, bit a huge chunk out of his Styrofoam cup.)

"We never dance in the mall." (Said when our daughter Annie, at age five, skipped and twirled from store to store, knocking products from the shelves and small children to the floor.)

For us, it must have been a genetic thing. We came by this honestly. When he was ten years old, Greg's family was on vacation, and as they drove through a small town in central Texas, Dad made an abrupt stop. Greg was in the middle of drinking directly from a large thermos full of ice water and, as a result of the sudden stop, managed to spill the entire contents of the jug, soaking himself and the entire backseat. "Don't you know that you never drink water in town?" was Dad's flustered reaction.

We might have been too embarrassed to confess our failures to you, except for the fact that, when we started to talk to our friends about it, we discovered that we weren't any different than anybody else. They had a few doozies of their own that they shared with us.

"You didn't ask me for any advice, so I won't give you much." (It doesn't really make sense, but we like it!)

"Oh, girls, NO! The baby doesn't like peanuts!" (As the five-year-old twins tried to feed peanuts to their three-week-old sister.)

"Vaseline wasn't made for cats!" (Never leave a cat, a jar of petroleum jelly, and a kid who's supposed to be taking a nap in a room together. This is what you'll get, we can almost assure you.)

"Stop hitting each other in the heads with your hammers!" (Remind Santa never to bring two little boys tool kits for Christmas. And another question: Are there any other areas that are off-limits as targets?)

"You'll never get the car with that attitude!" (Nice long-range strategy by a dad to his seven-year-old.)

"That's exactly what I'm talking about!" (One mom was known to blurt this same line out whenever things got out of hand. Never mind that there hadn't been any previous discussion of the topic.)

"A tar ball is not a toy." (But it looks like so much fun!)

"If you are going to jump on the bed, at least get in the middle." (Sounds like this mom has pretty much given up hope of regaining control here.)

"Don't eat that ice after it's been in your pants!" (We really don't want to know any more of the details except that we heard a dad say it to his son, age four, at a soccer game.)

When we're blindsided by things that we never expected to happen, sometimes our parental response only adds to the chaos. This happens in every family from time to time, but when chaos becomes the norm, when confusion becomes the reality, the entire home can collapse into a complete mess. Then "There's always something" becomes "How are we ever going to deal with this?" as the little disruptions get bigger and bigger. They become more critical than those earlier "We'll look back on this and laugh" moments with which we were once confronted.

Proverbs 29:18 is a familiar verse of Scripture, a warning to an unnamed group of people about an indefinite fate as a result of uncertain failures. We're probably most familiar with the King James translation: "Where there is no vision, the people perish."

The whole thing sounds ominous, to say the least. It certainly seems like it might be talking about death and destruction, and that's definitely serious. But wouldn't those severe consequences only be reserved for an entire nation who had departed from their faith in God, or a church that had drifted from its calling? How could it have anything to do with what goes on in the home?

Let's study this Scripture in a bit more detail. Actually, let's examine just one word—*perish*. According to *Strong's Hebrew Dictionary of the Bible*, and many other more current Bible translations, the original Hebrew word used there could more accurately be defined as "out of control" or "unrestrained." Now, does that sound a little more familiar? Despite our best efforts, at some point, every home could be described just like that. And we've all experienced that, during those hectic times, nothing good is going to be accomplished. We just hope to put the fire out before it overwhelms everyone in the family. We decide that we can deal with the damage later. Usually that's the way it goes. We recover, everything is forgiven and forgotten, and everyone is back on track again.

But what happens in the home where there's no concept of stability to rally around? Or, suppose one catastrophe is immediately followed by another . . . and another . . . and another? That's a situation Proverbs 29:18 might label "unrestrained" or "out of control." The result is that the kids usually rebel, and often the adults in that family either withdraw or react emotionally, causing even more stress followed by more chaos. That home is perishing and in need of help.

The scary thing is that no family is exempt. Unrestrained, if it's left unchecked, can become chaotic even in "good" homes. And, at the very least, an unrestrained family is missing out on the fulfillment and joy that results from living out God's purposes. It robs each member of the family of confidence and security. And the impact of that family upon their world is diluted.

Vision changes things, though. We can make that assumption because our verse in Proverbs tells us that the lack of it is what causes the messes in the first place. When our family is led by God's vision, we discover and achieve his calling as a group. A home with vision deals with difficulty wisely, and it can overcome setbacks. The individuals under that roof are more likely to stay on track, and it's much easier for them to find their way back if they do stray. Your family's vision is your front window to the rest of the world. Vision, or the lack of it, defines who you are. It's how you see yourselves and your world, and it's how the world sees you.

So vision might just be the cure-all for every problem we have at home, right? Probably not, only because we're still dealing with a houseful of imperfect people at our house, and in yours. Just like it happens with individuals, a family might drift from God's purposes from time to time. But we think vision is so important to building your family's foundation of faith that it deserves our writing this book about it. And we believe it's important to God that we investigate the principles of Proverbs 29:18 and apply them in the context of our homes. In the following chapters, we'll discover just what vision really is and how it might look in each aspect of your family's life.

Your family might be in chaos right now. You're desperate for a radical change and new direction. Finding God's vision immediately is crucial for you, and we pray that you'll find answers in his promise. Then again, things may be rolling along pretty smoothly at the moment in your home. And, as nice as that might seem, when comfort becomes the thing that you're willing to settle for, you'll miss out on the discovery of God's great adventure of faith for your family. We believe that, through his vision, he offers refreshment and new life for everyone under your roof. Vision brings focus and fulfillment to what your family does and how they think. It creates an atmosphere in your home in which each person can realize his or her potential in God. It sets your family and each individual member of your household on a course of action. And the whole world is watching it happen.

FOCUS

What do you think is the difference between a day when organization goes out the window, and a situation where a family is truly in chaos?

If you would characterize your family situation as chaotic right now, what would you be willing to do, as an individual or as a couple, to try to change that?

If things are going along smoothly, what are some reasons you might want to step out of your family's comfort zone?

Chapter Two

What Vision Isn't

There's another important word in Proverbs 29:18 that we're sure you were hoping we'd get to. What, exactly, is this "vision" thing we're talking about? As it stands alone, the word sounds somewhat mystical and ethereal. But if it weren't dealing with something very relevant and practical, then it certainly wouldn't be worth investing valuable family time on. We could call on some theologians and Hebrew scholars at this point to deconstruct the verse and redefine the word for us. We're just not sure that would be the best way to understand what vision really is. And since that's what this book is about, it's important for us to find a practical and useful definition of the word, right at the beginning.

There are quite a few religious words, like *faith* and *grace*, that are hard to define. Because vision isn't a concrete thing that we can see or touch, each of our definitions might be clouded by our personal perspective and experiences. So, first, let's narrow the field a bit by defining what vision is not.

Vision isn't a goal. Goal-oriented people get things done. Because they're focused on their goals, they complete tasks and gain a lot of ground on everyone else because they know what they want, and they go after it. If you've ever spent a significant amount of time around people who are driven by their goals, they can either intimidate you or inspire you.

Have you ever known people who achieved their goals, but they were headed in the wrong direction? What happens to people who push hard to accomplish things, only to find emptiness when they discover all that ambition was misguided? They accomplish one goal after another but never feel the real fulfillment they had expected. Then either they lose all perspective and work themselves to an early grave, or they give up, hopeless and disappointed.

Those are the people who set goals and push toward them but have no vision. The things they strive for don't necessarily match up with what God has intended for them, so their goals are empty. God's vision guides goals. A person with vision is able to set goals wisely, and the things he or she achieves bring fulfillment and gratification. A family led by a godly vision, that sets goals as a group and achieves them, changes their world. They inspire each other, and everyone inside their home tastes the sweetness of fulfillment.

Vision is more timeless than any goal, even a long-term one. It introduces God's point of view into achievement and success. Because he sees things in an eternal perspective, God's vision allows us to streamline our effort and make every task effective.

Vision isn't a dream. Dreamers might be the exact opposite of those people who are goal-driven. Many people, especially those high-octane achievers, might look down their noses at dreamers, because dreamers' approach to life is often a bit different from that of most other people. They're often seen as people with their heads in the clouds, somewhat impractical and ethereal. But dreamers are the people who have creative ideas and bring new perspectives to issues. If people build on a dream, they often persevere through difficulties, because their dream provides something to which they can look forward.

But there's a caution to those who merely imagine, because a dream very often remains just a dream. Standing alone, it never matures beyond a pleasant fantasy. Sometimes these people might allow their dreams to become so distant from reality that they, in fact, can never be anything more than simply dreamers rather than doers.

Vision is based on reality. A dream that is born from vision is factual and achievable, because it factors in strengths and weaknesses and circumstances and situations. Vision pulls dreams away from a fantasy world, then it purifies them and makes them relevant without sapping the excitement from them. While a dream might remain dormant within the dreamer's mind, vision requires action. Vision never frustrates, like dreams often do, but it always fulfills.

In your home, vision will bring each person individually and your family as a whole the confidence to dream big dreams. Vision is God's truth, blended with the creativity that God's Spirit breathes within you. It produces in your home the boldness and fearlessness to step out in faith and act on your dreams.

Vision isn't purpose. The book *The Purpose Driven Life* has had a significant impact on millions of Christians over the past decade and more. The truths that pastor Rick Warren imparted there were so powerful that even many nonbelievers embraced them, too. In the book, Pastor Warren essentially defines *purpose* as "becoming what God created you to be." Contentment and effectiveness are found in walking in God's purpose for our lives.

But in order for us to discover our purpose as individuals and as families, vision is necessary. Vision helps us to determine and define what our purpose is, because it allows us to accurately assess the entirety of who we are. Vision includes not only our God-given gifts and abilities but also the place and circumstances in which we find ourselves. Vision leads us to the directions we should pursue and to the people God has placed in our lives. In a purpose-driven family, the individuals in it might or might not know what their purpose is or where they fit in. Vision defines that for everyone.

Vision isn't hope. A number of years ago, the UCLA Bruins football team came to Austin, Texas, as clear underdogs to face the seventh-ranked Texas Longhorns. The Bruins' excitement and anticipation about the season had been beaten down by a rash of injuries and some bad breaks. Then, when they lost their first two games in the schedule, they seemed to forget what it took to win.

Their coach that year was a friend of ours, Rick Neuheisel, and he knew that this was a crucial game not just for the season, but for the future of his UCLA program. After Texas took a 3–0 lead in the first quarter, Neuheisel's Bruins scored 20 unanswered points and never looked back. They stunned the Longhorns 34–12. In the postgame interview, Rick acknowledged that his team had played the first two games of the season just hoping they would win. "Hope," said Coach Neuheisel, "isn't a very good strategy."[1]

Hope is necessary in every human being's life. Without it, people wither, and they can't find any reason to continue whatever they began. But Coach Neuheisel was exactly right—hope is not a good strategy. It won't provide a foundation because it's based on what might be or what could be. Hope is dependent on outside forces in order to become reality.

What makes hope a good thing, then? When it is clearly defined within the context of vision and faith, it becomes a powerful motivator. Hebrews 11:1 confirms that "Faith is the confidence that what we hope for will actually happen; it gives us assurance about things we cannot see" (NLT 2007).

Without vision, knowing who God is and how he works in us and through us, faith is empty. And without faith, hope becomes shallow. Since vision is based on God's perspective and God's wisdom, hope can sustain us, not in our own strength or abilities, but in his grace, love, and power.

Every home will inevitably face difficulties, and sometimes those rough places may even appear to be insurmountable. A family with vision remains hopeful, because they know the One they serve, the Source of all they have, all they are, and all they can be.

Vision isn't a plan. Our family has always loved to plan vacations. In fact, some people have speculated that the Griswold family of the *Vacation* movie series was actually modeled after us. That's just not true. Our plans are much more successful than theirs. We will admit, however, that on any trip we have taken, business or pleasure, we were careful to bring along *the notebook.* It's full of strategies, ideas, coupons, and directions that we are certain will make our entire trip more pleasurable and stress-free.

We learned early in our lives, though, that our plans don't always fall into place as neatly as we expect. One of our first vacation disasters occurred when we pulled up to the place where we'd be spending the night on a trip into the mountains of New Mexico. We're not sure where they took those pictures posted on their website, but the large log cabin, featuring a wide covered porch complete with a swing, set on the side of a wooded mountain overlooking a stream running through a meadow where horses waited for riders wasn't anything near the reality.

The tiny log cabin we checked in to looked more like leftovers from the deserted mining camps we had seen and featured a small, steep step up to the door and only one window. The roof looked like the very next snowfall would cause the final cave-in. We stepped into our "quaint cabin nestled in the forest," and the first thing we noticed was the entire place was sitting at a definite angle, leaning so hard toward the back right-hand corner that it was actually difficult for us to stand up. And there was the distinct odor of gas escaping from the oven in the kitchen. Sitting on that stove was an iron skillet containing coagulated grease topped by a good half-inch of dust.

As we carried in our luggage, Matt looked into the cabin through a large knothole in the wall, and Annie asked in a panicked voice if we thought bugs could get in through the hole. As the smell of gas grew stronger, we realized that there was a good possibility we wouldn't survive the night, so we reloaded our gear, and we got out of there. Fast. We were "off notebook" and had to scramble to find other accommodations, but that turned out to be one of our favorite trips, and the story of the cabin has been told and retold with much laughter, until it has become an epic family tale.

Planning is a good thing. It's a lot of fun for families to plan activities together, and good planning can save you a lot of money and a lot of time. But plans can also paralyze you. You can become a prisoner to rigid planning that causes you to miss out on the serendipitous things that life has to offer you. Rather than being a road map, vision is more like a compass that keeps you headed in the right direction.

A godly vision allows you to adjust to what happens in your life. When you're rigid about your plans, they can enslave you, and they can rob you of joy. But plans that fall apart are rescued if our first priority is depending on an overriding vision. That vision within your home creates an atmosphere where the family can deal with disappointments. It brings your lives into focus with God's perspective on difficulties that stand in your way.

In the New Testament, when James wrote about trouble and disappointment, his point of view seemed almost unbelievable. But because the foundation of his focus was a godly vision, that unusual perspective was real and alive in him. "Dear brothers and sisters," he wrote, "when troubles of any kind come your way, consider it an opportunity for great joy. For you know that when your faith is tested, your endurance has a chance to grow. So let it grow, for when your endurance is fully developed, you will be perfect and complete, needing nothing" (James 1:2–4).

Vision makes room for grace within your home. Plans aren't the only thing that can fall apart in a family. People can, too. And when those plans for someone's perfect future are shattered by wrong choices or unforeseen circumstances, a family with vision can rethink and readjust, bringing healing and restoration into that loved one's life, and into the whole family.

We're hoping that by narrowing it down a bit, you're beginning to understand a little more clearly what vision is. But you're probably not any closer to making it a reality in your home. So just be patient and keep reading. We're going to further clarify a family's vision and show you how it can happen practically and effectively for you.

Focus

If you have ever set out a defined purpose, or specific goals, list them.

Think of the successes you have had in fulfilling the points on your list. Consider the times when something, either internal or external, may have thrown you off track. What effect did setbacks have on your family?

Chapter Three

What Vision Is

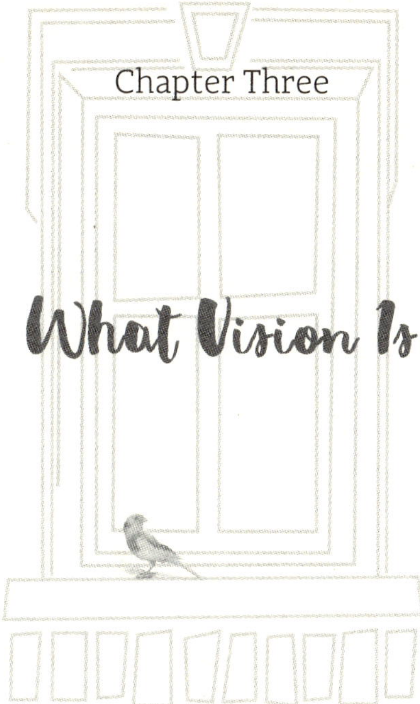

Football legend Mike Singletary is one of our family's heroes. When he was a freshman at Baylor University, we saw him perform on the field and knew then he was destined for greatness. He was a star with the Chicago Bears, was selected as a member of the Pro Football Hall of Fame, and placed fifty-sixth on the 1999 *Sporting News* list of one hundred greatest football players.

Just how deep does our fanaticism for Mike go? When our son, Matt, was in graduate school at Baylor University, he was on staff at a thriving church that was made up of mostly college students. One of his responsibilities was meeting with freshmen who had visited the church in order to connect them with where they might serve in the church's ministries. He called us one day, excited and out of breath, exclaiming, "I just met Mike Singletary's daughter for lunch, but I felt really awkward when I blurted out, 'I have your dad's jersey hanging on my bedroom wall!'"

The intensity Mike displayed as a star linebacker is only surpassed by his intensity in serving Christ and his dedication to his family. The Singletarys are a family of vision. Mike and his wife, Kim, inspired us with a creed that they wrote for their family.

> This is the home of champions. As Singletarys, we will always strive to do our very best in all we do. We will strive to be honest and respect each other's feelings, property and time. We will always pray for one another, fight for one another and encourage one another. For our trust be not in our home, nor our money or status or knowledge, but in each other, and above all, in our Lord and Savior Jesus Christ.[1]

The Singletarys' vision defined who they are and how they approach life. It was painted broadly enough to address almost any situation that would come up in their home, but it was precise enough to give scarcely any misunderstanding or wiggle room. Their family creed was carefully thought through and precisely spelled out. Word for word, they spelled out God's vision for their family.

Discovering a practical, effective vision for your family requires a clear understanding of what a vision is *not* and, more importantly, what it *is*. A family vision requires some specific framework in order for it to be authentic and workable.

Vision is God-given. The thing that separates vision from other plans and ideas you might have for your family is that it's not about *your* plans and ideas at all. Vision is God's perspective lived in and through your family's everyday life. In Genesis, he created Adam and Eve, made them a family, and gave them a vision for their mission. Just like that first family in the Garden of Eden, your family was God's idea, and he has a purpose for its existence and a mission for you to accomplish. His vision for who your family is guides you, together, toward that purpose and that mission.

It's doubtful that too many people would consider comedian Woody Allen a theologian or a spiritual icon. He is the one, though, who is credited with one of the most insightful thoughts about God's perspective. "If you want to make God laugh," he said, "tell him your plans." God, in all of his love for us, would probably not be so dismissive of our thoughts and ideas as Woody Allen assumes. But this quote about the Almighty One reveals plenty about how we sometimes think the course of our lives should go. Have you ever fallen into the trap of doing things the way you think they should be done, taking for granted that God will fall into step with you? To live out God's vision in our homes, we need to intentionally seek *his* plans and *his* direction, first of all and above all.

Vision is foundational. In defining what vision was not, we saw that goals, dreams, purpose, hope, and plans are all good things, but they all require vision in order to maximize their effectiveness. Vision is what makes them all work in a family's life. In finding God's vision for your family and then in living it out, you have to believe that his vision for you is at the epicenter of everything else in your family's life. It provides the foundation for who you are and the decisions you make. Building on that foundation, your family's framework takes a more definite shape.

As you align your family's life to God's vision, choices become more clear-cut. Rules and expectations have a reason and a purpose. They don't stand alone. Vision becomes the motivation for good behavior and selfless serving, because it expresses who God wants your family to be to the world around you. Vision defines your family's mission, and it gives each member confidence to walk the journey of faith.

Vision is unique. It just makes sense that if God took so much care to make each person within your family unique, then your entire family's vision will be different from those of other families. God's vision for your family will consider the strengths and weaknesses that are unique to your family as a whole. These mesh with the talents and abilities of each family member, creating a patchwork design that is unlike what any other family has to offer.

Vision is inclusive. You've probably observed a family before and labeled one person the "black sheep." While everyone else seems to be in sync with each other, this poor soul doesn't seem to fit in. He's obviously different, marching to the beat of a different drummer. Too often that loner strays, isolating himself from the rest of the family. If the rest of the family doesn't step in to bring him back, he could drift further and further away.

True godly vision is broad enough to include everyone in your family. As you discover your family's vision, one of the challenges will be to extend it in every direction so that everyone knows his or her role and plays a part in who your family is.

Diversity is a strength because it broadens your experiences and your impact on the world in which God placed you. But diversity is only effective when it's included as a vital part of the whole. In your family, every individual has a purpose toward making you all you're intended to be.

Vision is active. If your vision doesn't include action, it just won't last. It withers, loses its impact, and becomes sterile and uninteresting. As you discover what God intends your family to be, you have to accompany that abstract vision with projects that give it life and reality. That is the real reason that your family exists. The satisfaction that comes from fulfilling your vision builds, develops, and creates more opportunities for your family to reach out.

Action fuels the fire of vision. Watching every member participate and accomplish real things is stimulating. And action requires more action. It sets the mark for the future, allowing your family to dream bigger dreams.

Vision is eternal. When God is the source of your family's vision, you will soon realize that it's intended to survive far beyond the days of young children at home. Vision provides the foundation for the character of every family member, now and for generation after generation. It's your legacy. Your family's vision puts an indelible stamp on each life that follows, and each person must choose whether to make it a part of his or her life.

That's why, when you're formulating your family's vision, you have to understand that it's seen through a wide-angle lens, a big-picture perspective. It's never narrow and temporary. Although it may change somewhat with circumstances or locales, it's focused on the eternal, things that God says are everlasting. Jesus gave us the right focus for our family vision:

> Don't store up treasures here on earth, where moths eat them and rust destroys them, and where thieves break in and steal. Store your treasures in heaven, where moths and rust cannot destroy, and thieves do not break in and steal. Wherever your treasure is, there the desires of your heart will also be. (Matt. 6:19–21)

As your family discovers the unique vision God has for you, you'll understand how he has placed you and gifted you. And as you join together as a family to work and serve others, you'll find that each part of your family carries out their unique responsibilities and completes the whole picture. You'll be amazed at how carefully he brought your family together and at the beauty he intends to demonstrate to your world through you.

Focus

What legacies might you identify in your family from the families of your parents and grandparents?

Whether godly or otherwise, what attitudes toward other family members, and toward those outside the family, are being repeated in your home?

Part Two

Looking in Your Window

Chapter Four

Finding That "Perfect" Family

Let's suppose you were just appointed to head up a very important project. Your job is to find families that can be entrusted to effectively demonstrate to the world God's work and his way of doing things. Obviously, you'll be considering only the cream of the crop, the very best of the best. You've been presented a stack of resumes that you will review and, first of all, you'll reject the ones that have no chance of being considered. What would you do with the following candidates?

Family #1

Dad is not a believer, and Mom and Grandma have the sole responsibility of creating an atmosphere in the home in which the son's faith can grow. They have taken charge in that area, and they are quite insistent on making it happen. There is, no doubt, quite a bit of conflict and distance that exists within this family.

Family #2

Dad was a deceitful man, and his first marriage was terrible. But he and wife number one have seven children together. He also has four sons out of wedlock with two other women. Finally, he married the love of his life and has two children with her. His ten oldest boys, though, hate the two youngest ones, especially the eleventh son, because he is obviously Dad's favorite. They try everything they can to make that son miserable, and they actually tried to get rid of him at one point. The two wives battle also, and Dad seems very weak in his attempts to keep things under control.

Family #3

Mom was at one time a prostitute. Apparently, she is quite well-known as such in her hometown. Dad is probably one of her former customers, but of course no one knows that for sure except the two of them. But people whisper. When her age began to lessen her beauty, and cut into her business, she retired from the profession and married him. They have one son, who is now an adult, and despite his upbringing, he is quite successful in real estate.

Family #4

Mom had her first child out of wedlock when she was just a teenager. She had an amazing story about how it happened, and when she told people about it, few believed her. Even though he knew he wasn't the baby's father, her boyfriend married her anyway. At one point, when they were on a road trip, Mom and Dad forgot their twelve-year-old son and had to backtrack to go find him.

You've probably already figured out the true identities of these four families, but in case you're not certain, we'll tell you whose resumes you've been holding.

Family #1

Timothy's Family

In his letter to Timothy, Paul mentioned the young man's mother, Eunice, and his grandmother, Lois. Paul was Timothy's mentor and recognized that, despite some difficult situations in his home and with no help from his father, he had a strong spiritual foundation and was prepared to reach out to his world with his message of faith (2 Tim. 1:5).

Family #2

Jacob's Family

Jacob's twelve sons became the twelve tribes of Israel, fulfilling the promise that God had made to him. He had a history of trying to make things happen rather than relying on God, and that brought him a lot of pain and heartache. Still, God used Jacob to father a nation. Despite his failures as a father and a husband, his son, Joseph, a mighty man of God, was chosen by God to rescue Israel and to guide them in the ways of his Heavenly Father (Gen. 25–50).

Family #3

Rahab's Family

Most of us are a bit timid and somewhat hesitant when we discuss the fact that a prostitute is one of Jesus's ancestors. But Rahab rescued the Israelite spies who had been sent into the Promised Land, and as a result, God redeemed her and used her in his story. She married a man named Salmon, and they had a son named Boaz. We know Rahab taught her son one valuable lesson. Boaz, like his mother did with the spies, reached out to two immigrants, Ruth and Naomi, and rescued them when they were in need (Josh. 2; Ruth 1–4).

Family #4

Jesus's Family

When Jesus was born to Mary and Joseph, it wasn't in the midst of the most pleasant circumstances. Besides the fact that the baby was born in a manger, there were still social and cultural issues that needed to be addressed regarding her pregnancy. In addition to that, King Herod was set on destroying the life of this Child because of the talk that he was the Messiah. And yes, there was the time that Mary and Joseph thought Jesus was with some of the others in their group as they traveled back home. But he had

Who's Your Favorite TV Family?

Since the 1950s, Americans have formed some of their ideas about family life from television. As we've watched our favorite on-screen families from week to week, we've often seen them as the family we'd like to be or, sometimes, the family that we closely resembled. We took a quick poll of our Facebook friends and asked them who their favorite TV family was. We got some interesting responses. I suppose that would be because we have some interesting friends!

FAMILY	SHOW	PERCENTAGE
Waltons	*The Waltons*	11.48%
Huxtables	*The Cosby Show*	10.17%
Ingalls	*Little House on the Prairie*	7.38%
Andersons	*Father Knows Best*	4.92%
Taylors	*Andy Griffith Show*	4.92%
Cleavers	*Leave It to Beaver*	4.92%
Cartwrights	*Bonanza*	4.92%
Ricardos	*I Love Lucy*	4.01%
Petries	*The Dick Van Dyke Show*	3.28%
Cunninghams	*Happy Days*	2.46%
Keatons	*Family Ties*	2.46%
Crawleys	*Downton Abbey*	2.46%

remained in the temple in Jerusalem, and they had to return to the city to find him (Luke 2).

In both the Old and New Testaments, we read about how God worked in and through the lives of many imperfect families—people who didn't quite have it all together and whose public images might have been questionable. He used single parent families, blended families, and even divided families. God's grace and the willingness of these families to serve him combined to create families that the Lord used in authoring his story.

FAMILY	SHOW	PERCENTAGE
Bradys	*The Brady Bunch*	2.46%
Reagans	*Blue Bloods*	2.46%
Bunkers	*All in the Family*	2.46%
Belchers	*Bob's Burgers*	1.64%
Banks	*Fresh Prince of Bel-Air*	1.64%
Bravermans	*Parenthood*	1.64%
Connors	*Roseanne*	1.64%
Jeffersons	*The Jeffersons*	1.64%
Camdens	*Seventh Heaven*	1.64%
Dunphys	*Modern Family*	1.64%
Bowers	*Who's the Boss?*	1.64%
Taylors	*Home Improvement*	1.64%
Griffins	*Family Guy*	1.64%
Winslows	*Family Matters*	0.82%
Goldbergs	*The Goldbergs*	0.82%
Hecks	*The Middle*	0.82%
Barones	*Everybody Loves Raymond*	0.82%
Johnsons	*Black-ish*	0.82%
Thatchers	*Life Goes On*	0.82%
Gilmores	*The Gilmore Girls*	0.82%
Nelsons	*Adventures of Ozzie & Harriet*	0.82%
Posts	*Mr. Ed*	0.82%
Lawrences	*Family*	0.82%
Seavers	*Growing Pains*	0.82%
Douglases	*My Three Sons*	0.82%
Jetsons	*The Jetsons*	0.82%

Thankfully, that hasn't changed. In our culture today, families can look very different from what has been considered traditional. Circumstances can cause a variety of situations where a family is nothing like the old television sitcoms where everything was so perfect and polished. Then there are those more recent TV families who are such a complete mess that you might be identifying more with them at this point.

God understands every home's environment, the strengths and the weaknesses there, and his grace will not allow any family to be excluded. Wherever you are, and in whatever circumstance you find yourself, God will use your family. That's what his grace is all about, not only in the lives of each individual but in every household, too.

In order to experience this fulfillment in your home, you need to pay attention to his leading and make yourselves totally available to what he wants to do and how he wants to work with you. You surrender your plans and goals to God's plan for your family. At that point, you will begin to discover his unique vision for your family. Then you have to commit yourself to making it happen.

This is not a book for or about superheroes. We don't have to get "good enough" to be a family of vision. We don't have to appear to be a certain way that makes everyone around us comfortable. He wants each person under your roof, and all of you together as one unit, to be looking to him to do something there. Now, today, in the middle of your circumstances, is where God wants to begin working in you and with you.

Focus

Ask this conversation-making question of each member of your family, adjusting the wording to fit the age level of each person: What do you think we can do in order to be a family to each other? What do you need from the rest of us? How can we be a family, but still be open to positive relationships we each may have with relatives outside of this household?

Find a recording of the song *Come As You Are* by David Crowder. Consider making this a theme song for your family; it presents a message of God's grace and hope that you can share with all those around you.

Chapter Five

What Does Your Family Look Like?

If we had been assigned the job of creating families, we would probably have done things a lot differently than God did. We most likely would have inserted some kind of microchip in each person to ensure they all would be on the same track. Everybody would be in agreement about everything, and there would be total peace and harmony in the home. With none of the usual internal distractions, so much would be accomplished.

But God's idea was completely different. He created a group of distinctly different beings, with their own exclusive thoughts, ideas, motivations, abilities, likes, dislikes, and opinions. And he put them together under one roof, and called them a family. The beauty of each family is that it's a colorful combination of individuals. Our way of creating a family would be narrow and bland. God's way offers diverse personalities and unlimited opportunities.

From the very beginning, God has had a special mission for each family. He revealed his plans for Adam and Eve right after he created them. He told them to be fruitful and multiply, to tend the Garden of Eden and look after the animals. That seems rather simple compared to the complexity of the world we live in. After Adam and Eve understood their vision and began their mission, there was that one day the serpent approached Eve. He told her there was another way to get this done. If they listened to him, they could be like God. Now wouldn't that be better than just being the family God wanted them to be?

Since that time, as culture changed and each new family was formed, God has had a reason for every one of them to exist. In the same way that each individual has been commissioned by God with a distinct calling, each family has also had a particular purpose. One of the primary reasons families have been sidetracked is that either they never discovered their vision, or they tried to become something other than what they were intended to be.

Investigating God's Vision for Your Family

In order to experience the fulfillment of becoming everything God intended you to be, you're required to actually discover his unique vision for your family. Then you have to commit yourself to making it happen. The process is purposeful. God made you exactly who you are, and now it's your opportunity to become exactly who he made you to be.

So, let's get this started. It all begins with some good detective work on your part. When you discover who your family really is and what makes every individual tick, you will start to understand God's purpose for putting you all under the same roof. There are some basic things you'll have to do to be a good investigator.

Be Observant

It's so easy to fall into a parental autopilot mode. When everything at the house is running smoothly and complaints are at a minimum, we tend to lose our focus. But we signed up for a job that calls for complete involvement. Certainly, there are other responsibilities that will require our attention. But, during those times, we don't have the option of losing touch with what's going on at home.

Observing your family calls for that kind of continual commitment. During day-to-day living in your home, there are events, situations, and circumstances that call for your special attention.

- Study your family's best times and worst times, and analyze the processes that got you there. Discover each family member's role and reaction during those times.
- Create opportunities for nonthreatening family meetings. These aren't times for airing out grievances and pointing fingers, but you can have all-inclusive discussions about how life is going for everyone.
- Look for moments when family members demonstrate unity and teamwork. Evaluate the motivations that made it happen, and be sure to reward everyone for their good work.
- Keep an eye on each family member. Make note of the situations that cause them to struggle. Encourage them when they seem to be on a downslide.
- Find the places of commonality in your family. Observe those occasions when everyone is having a great time, or when everyone is working together. In each of those times, find the common denominators, the aspects that made them noteworthy.

The task of being observant at home can seem overwhelming at times. But it's great to know that you don't have to do it all alone. "If you need wisdom, ask our generous God, and he will give it to you. He will not rebuke you for asking" (James 1:5).

Ask God to show you his perspective and insight into the personality of your family and each person who's a part of it. You don't need to expect that he'll overwhelm you with a sudden burst of inspiration. Instead, you'll most likely simply be more aware of your family. Then you'll notice you have a new, clearer understanding of who they are and just what makes them tick.

Be Objective

Did you ever want something so much that you could actually visualize it?

Sometimes, we're so eager to have a great family that we tend to overlook who we really are. It's a universal hurdle that Paul addresses in Romans 12.

> Because of the privilege and authority God has given me, I give each of you this warning: Don't think you are better than you really are. Be honest in your evaluation of yourselves, measuring yourselves by the faith God has given us. Just as our bodies have many parts and each part has a special function, so it is with Christ's body. We are many parts of one body, and we all belong to each other. (Rom. 12:3–5)

An honest, objective view of our family is necessary to know what our family's vision is. Every family is a combination of strengths and weaknesses. The strengths, of course, are the foundations that we can build our vision on. But the weaknesses aren't necessarily hindrances to us.

In 2 Corinthians 12:9, Paul discusses the things that had, at one time, held him back from doing and being God's best. "Each time he [God] said, 'My grace is all you need. My power works best in weakness.' So now I am glad to boast about my weaknesses, so that the power of Christ can work through me." When, as a family, we learn where we're weak and then discover how we can allow God to be at work in those areas, our vision and our mission are only enhanced.

How can we be certain that we're seeing our family with a clear, unbiased point of view? Too often we overlook the simplest ways to get a good start on making those objective evaluations of our family.

Listen to Your Family

What do the people in your home have to say about their family experience? Inevitably, they will talk honestly about the things that give them a lot of happiness and fulfillment as well as the things they struggle with. You don't have to pry these things out of them, but you do have to listen and be aware of what they say. The conversation is normally going to be more on the surface rather than deep thoughts. After you hear someone else's comments, it's your job to analyze them and determine what they really mean. Are they coming from a place of joy and contentment or hurt and anger? Is the person feeling loved and supported or isolated and alone? As you weigh all these things, you likely will begin to uncover what each person, as well as your family as a whole, is really all about.

There's a creek that runs right behind our house. It's not a particularly special creek. It only has water in it after a nice rain has fallen in the area. It's just a place that has lots of big oak trees and huge limestone boulders. But when you're there, you feel a million miles away from the rest of the world. Since the time he was about two, Josiah, our now eight-year-old grandson, has loved it when G-Diddy (Greg) accompanies him to the creek. They throw rocks there, climb the creek banks, and push old dead logs around. In the middle of the creek bed, there's a short tree stump that they call Memory Stick, where they talk about the good times our family has had together. What Josiah says there reflects a lot of things that have been meaningful to him. So Greg has learned to listen. One particular boulder is large and rectangular, looking something like a park bench, that they named the Talking Rock. They sit down there and do just that—talk. There are no electronic interruptions, just the two guys talking about "stuff." Sometimes it's deep, like Josiah's thoughts about having cystic fibrosis, or bullies at school. More recently, the conversation is sometimes about . . . GIRLS!

When he visits our house, Josiah will often come to his grandpa and say, "G, can we go to the creek?" The two of them stroll down there, and they still throw rocks, explore the banks, and push logs around. And sometimes an eight-year-old boy reaches deep within himself and shares what he's thinking, what he's fearing, or what he's hurting over. When he first started taking Josiah to the creek, Greg just intended it to be a fun place. And, often, that's exactly what it is. But now he knows that if Josiah asks to go to the creek, he should be prepared to listen, too.

During the last few months, our two-year-old grandson, Levi, pulls Greg's hand and says, "Creek, G!" Right now, they're just throwing rocks and exploring the area. But Greg is listening.

Listen to Others

What do the people who are closest to your family say about who you are? When you're being a listener within your own home, you do just that—listen. And you don't need to ask any probing questions. But you can be a bit more proactive when you seek the input and evaluation of people who aren't living under your roof. Tell your extended family, your friends, or your pastor that you've determined to build a more focused and effective atmosphere in your home. What is their overall viewpoint of your family? Where can you be stronger? What do you do really well?

Be prepared for their answers, though. Sometimes it's not easy to take criticism, even if it's constructive, and even if it's something you asked for. Like most conversations with the people who are closest to you, you have to listen with a lot of grace and love. No fair getting upset or hurt when you've asked for an honest opinion. No fair trying to argue with them or disagree with what they say.

After you've gathered all this raw family data, it's time for the prayerful evaluation that Romans 12 talks about. First, write down your honest thoughts, with no justifications or alterations, rather than filtering them through your thinking process. Then, prayerfully put the pieces together to determine just who you are. Don't use other families as a measuring stick, because they're not exactly like you. Don't gloss over the blemishes, but don't sell your family short, either. God made something precious when he made your home.

Be Obedient

> For if you listen to the word and don't obey, it is like glancing at your face in a mirror. You see yourself, walk away, and forget what you look like. But if you look carefully into the perfect law that sets you free, and if you do what it says and don't forget what you heard, then God will bless you for doing it. (James 1:23–25)

After detectives gather all the information, there's one remaining step left to bring the process to a conclusion. And it happens to be the most important one of them all. They have to implement a plan of action from all the data that they've compiled.

When all your research is complete, your final step is to make those adjustments that will align your family's goals and priorities with God's vision. James 1 promises that when we commit to the changes that need to be made in our homes, we're allowing God to be involved. And that's when things begin to happen.

Each family's specific problem areas are just as unique as their talents and gifts. As you uncover the places where your family struggles, it's important to confront those difficulties and adjust your thinking and your actions to correct them. It never works to try to hide them or ignore them and hope they'll get better. When you make change a priority, God's light will bring life there.

Focus

Write down the names of each person in your family. List what you perceive as their interests, strengths, talents . . . and weaknesses.

Ask family members to brainstorm the answers to these questions: What is our family good at? Where do we need to improve?

Chapter Six

What Do Others See?

As you drive through a neighborhood in Anyplace, USA, and spot a house with the drapes on the front window wide open, do you ever get the urge to just peek in and see what's going on? We're not hinting at anything creepy here, but the fact is most people would be curious about what it's like inside. What's that family doing right now? How is their home decorated? What's their story?

What would people see if they looked through the front window of your home? We're not talking about the drapes and furniture, or whether or not the breakfast dishes are still in the sink. And perfection, or even an image that projects it, is not the goal we're seeking to fulfill under our roof. In fact, any manufactured image at all is very easy to see through, so it's no use to even try.

We're talking about reality. What reactions do people see when your family is under pressure? If others were asked to describe what your family is all about, what would they say? Would they have a tough time finding the right adjectives?

A family with a true vision for who they are can leave an unmistakable impression upon everyone around them. That's because when a family's vision is in place, they become much more than just the nice things they do. Their vision creates their character. That family actually *becomes* their vision. And if your vision is alive and active in your home, others will recognize it and readily point it out to you.

That's because those homes are easy to recognize. Their goals and actions line up with their vision. They are unified and responsive to one another. When they encounter difficult things, they don't fall apart. There is a recognizable peacefulness within the walls of their homes. As you watch life happen there, you notice that it all seems very genuine, too. The natural outgrowth of families guided by a vision is an observable personality that guides them and gives them a solid foundation.

Within the text of Jesus's Sermon on the Mount, he compares his followers to salt. When you sprinkle salt, it enhances the flavor of everything it comes in contact with. Our "saltiness" as a family of vision does the same. It *revitalizes* the stale places in the lives of those who are around us, in our neighborhoods, our workplaces, or our schools. Our vision, lived out through our family, encourages them to find what we have.

Now, this is where Proverbs 29:18 becomes so relevant. When a family lacks this vision, their noticeable traits become restlessness, confusion, and a lack of restraint. When you look through their window, you're likely to see these things, because a family that lacks vision seems to move from one troublesome time to another. Parents don't see the response they want from the kids, because the kids don't know exactly what is expected of them. Nobody in that household knows who they are as individuals, much less who their entire family is. If goals have been set for behavior or accomplishments, they're usually not fulfilled because there's no framework on which to build them.

Their lack of vision prevents them from finding a way to right themselves when the first wave of difficulty comes through. And then, each crisis that follows pushes them further away from a place where they can find safety and security, much less growth and fulfillment.

When a family has a God-inspired vision in place, all the family members know their role and their responsibilities. The kids don't have to constantly ask Mom or Dad "Why?" or "Do I have to?" because the reasons have already been established in your home. But when those moments do arise, it is much easier to give the kids an answer other than "Because I said so."

In 2012, when Robert Griffin III entered the National Football League, he inherited the starting quarterback position for the Washington Redskins. Added to the responsibility of performing his duties on the football field, Robert, as the team's quarterback, was also expected to assume a leadership role on a team full of veteran players. That was a huge task for the twenty-two-year-old, just out of Baylor University. One of the first things he did after signing with the Redskins inspired and challenged his teammates. On Twitter, Robert sent a message to all of them that read, simply, "Know your why." As his new teammates began to respond to his tweet, he dug deeper into what he wanted them to discover. He wanted to know why they were playing football for the Redskins, and what drove them as they played. His purpose was to build within his team accountability and unity.

Your challenge, as a parent, is to construct a why for your family and creatively instill it in each member's life. You teach it to them with family stories and through casual discussions and through asking them questions. You demonstrate it with family projects that reach out to others outside your home. You point it out when it serendipitously appears. You talk about it, again and again. That's how you cultivate a genuine vision for your family. It will begin to take root and then become who your family really is. Through your window, others won't see perfection. But they will observe character that they will desire in their homes, too.

In the rest of Part Two, we're going to discuss the practical, positive aspects of becoming a family with a vision, and developing your own definition of *why* for your family. Each of these attributes is like another flower pushing up through the ground and then beginning to bloom. The seeds are planted when you determine your vision and decide for certain that this is what you want your home to look like. But then you have to take care of each one of these characteristics, tending it, feeding it, and protecting it, so your vision will bear fruit.

What others see of your family, then, won't be just a pretty portrait, but it will be real, living-and-breathing life. As your family benefits from living out the attributes of your vision inside the home, each part and the entire vision become more and more evident because your family is walking within its true likeness. And from that the whole world benefits, too. Through the window, others see an attractive blending of people and personalities that they would desire in their own homes. They observe an authentic example that will affect what they can become, too. As the family lives out its vision, the rest of the world discovers the love of God in real flesh and blood.

Focus

What is the best thing you think people might see when they look at your family?

When everyone is together, at a meal or in the car, ask each person (who is old enough to do so) to write down their personal why, and what they think is your why as a family. Take turns sharing your answers.

Chapter Seven

Finding Unity through Your Vision

When we get a chance to sit down and watch television together, one of our favorites is the ABC series *The Middle*. It features the Heck family, middle-of-the-road folks, with a middle income, residing in middle America. The mom is Frankie, who narrates the stories, giving us an insight into her hopes and dreams. And then her panicky responses to the extreme chaos that always seems to occur push her desires for a perfect family even more out of sight. She has held down several jobs, including selling used cars and working as the receptionist in a dental office. Mike, the dad, is the foreman at a quarry, and though it's decent employment, the business is always on the edge of a temporary seasonal shutdown. He prides himself on being a guy who never shows any emotion. Their teenage son, Axl, is focused on girls, football, and being cool. Sue, the Hecks' daughter, is painfully awkward and unpopular, but always striving to be somebody. And then there's quirky Brick, the youngest son, who buries himself in books, often whispering to himself, and quite content with being overlooked by the rest of the family.

Except for the few moments when they're able to pull things together to the point of almost being successful at something, the Hecks are usually the victims of "whatever can go wrong, does go wrong." They each pursue their own path to what they think will bring happiness, but it never does. There would never be any unity in the Heck household if it weren't for the rare occasions when their individual frantic pursuits of happiness cause them to arrive at the same point at the same time.

Although the Hecks' lifestyle sounds tragic and extremely painful to watch, it's actually quite hilarious on a TV screen within the safety of your living room. You don't have to finish one episode to realize that this family has no vision. They each dive headfirst into life, without the stability and confidence that unity brings to a home.

As your family's vision grows, unity will follow. You don't have to concentrate on making your home unified. It's simply a natural outgrowth of people having a common foundation and purposes. In Romans 15:5, we can read about God's involvement in creating unity as a family's vision matures.

> May our dependably steady and warmly personal God develop maturity in you so that you get along with each other as well as Jesus gets along with us all. Then we'll be a choir—not our voices only, but our very lives singing in harmony in a stunning anthem to the God and Father of our Master Jesus! (*The Message*)

As we commit ourselves to the vision that God has for us, he is the One who brings about that growing unity in our homes. Paul compares it to being in a choir. A choir is made up of a variety of voices—sopranos, altos, tenors, and basses. Each one of them has a different part to sing, but they combine the variety of voices under the director's baton, and a beautiful, harmonious musical creation is the product.

That can happen in families, too. Like a choir, your home is made up of those different voices, and your vision is potentially like that musical composition. As all the parts rehearse the "music," the result is a harmonious home that appeals to everyone around you and brings glory to the Composer.

The Love Factor

If there is a commitment on our part to bring about unity in our families, it is necessary to make love a priority. Love doesn't just happen; it's a discipline. In wedding ceremonies, 1 Corinthians 13 is often read. In that context, it sounds so sweet and romantic. But the text isn't intended specifically for newlyweds. Here's a challenge for you: Can you live out the attributes of 1 Corinthians 13 love in your home? In the tough times, can you still commit yourself to it?

Love is the soil that allows unity to grow and flourish. It has always been foundational to God's work among his people. Jesus established it when he met with his family, the disciples, as they had the Last Supper. He gave specific instructions about the importance of love. "So now I am giving you a new commandment: Love each other. Just as I have loved you, you should love each other. Your love for one another will prove to the world that you are my disciples" (John 13:34–35).

Tertullian was a second-century Christian theologian, an avid defender of the faith. He was known for being a fiery challenger to the Romans' attacks on fellow believers. He studied the Romans and uncovered any advantages those early Christians had that would help them overcome the enemy's onslaught. He shared with those early Christians the one thing that absolutely baffled the

Romans: "What marks us in the eyes of our enemies is our loving kindness. 'Only look,' they say, 'look how they love one another.'"[1]

As in the second century, so it is now. When the world sees genuine love, it will take notice. Love becomes something that others desire to experience. There is nothing more attractive than selfless, giving love in action. And in our homes, when that same love is alive and evident, it works to strengthen the unity that is so vital there, too. Real love must be expressed. We don't get a pass because, like Mike Heck, we just don't show emotion. Even if vocal and visible expressions of love are difficult for us, we have to step out of our comfort zone to make certain that each member of the family knows, with absolutely no doubt, that they are loved.

There's a complete circle that's formed when all these characteristics are active in your home. The connection that love creates is the thing that sustains unity within the family. Then the unity that develops ensures a more peaceful place to live. And when you're creating your family's vision, peace and cooperation are necessary for it to thrive.

The Prayer Factor

As important as love and unity are to your vision, it's good to know that you don't have to stand alone and only hope that they begin to flourish. Jesus set a precedent of prayer in developing unity. Before his crucifixion, he petitioned his Father concerning those who were his followers.

> I pray that they will all be one, just as you and I are one—as you are in me, Father, and I am in you. And may they be in us so that the world will believe you sent me. I have given them the glory you gave me, so they may be one as we are one. I am in them and you are in me. May they experience such perfect unity that

> the world will know that you sent me and that you love them as much as you love me. (John 17:21–23)

Prayer is a vital part of encouraging and developing unity in your family. Not only should parents pray for each other and for the kids, but the entire family should join together to pray for each other. A special connection develops when someone hears her name being called out in a time of prayer. Making a family prayer time a priority will strengthen the harmony and solidarity in your home.

As you share your vision with the members of your family, and they begin to visualize their own concept of what it looks like, you'll see unity develop. Places where chaos once held your family in its grip will have a new light shining on them. Expect God's peace to begin to replace that mess.

> How wonderful, how beautiful,
> when brothers and sisters get along!
> It's like costly anointing oil
> flowing down head and beard,
> Flowing down Aaron's beard,
> flowing down the collar of his priestly robes.
> It's like the dew on Mount Hermon
> flowing down the slopes of Zion.
> Yes, that's where GOD commands the blessing,
> ordains eternal life.
>
> (Psalm 133 *The Message*)

Focus

In an effort to give family prayer time new life and relevance for each member, try one or two of the following activities.

Ask the members of the family what they want the others to pray for. Write the answers on a list, and post it where everyone can see.

Let each person write out the subject of his or her prayer on a sticky note, and stick them in places that people often see, or use dry-erase markers to write them on bathroom and bedroom mirrors.

Make each day of the week "Pray for [Family Member] Day" for a different family member. For example, you could give your daughter a note with your prayer for her written on it, send her a text, or go around the table speaking sentence prayers for her. At the end of the week, let each family member report back on what they learned or experienced because of it.

At whatever time the family is all together, let each person give "highs and lows" for the day (or the week, if that's more doable). This is a great way to know what to pray for, and how to offer encouragement to, each family member.

Chapter Eight

Finding Clarity through Your Vision

"Let me make this perfectly clear . . ." Whenever you hear that phrase, you anticipate that you're about to hear something very confusing. What will follow is a mishmash of meaningless words that attempt to restate or rearrange the facts in order to make the real truth easier to swallow. It's usually just a delaying tactic so the communicator can think of a way to explain something away. Politicians are famous for it, but professors and teachers are also guilty, as are flustered managers and supervisors and many others with some kind of authority. Even moms and dads have been known to utter the phrase to the kids while they try to think of what to do during a particularly stressful or confusing moment of parenting.

Making ourselves understood isn't a trivial matter, though, especially when it comes to our families. Things that are left unsaid or unexplained often are the very source of some of the most difficult situations in our home. We might assume that everybody understands, but too often, it turns out that we were completely wrong in that assumption. When events in our family unexpectedly veer off course, it's usually because somebody just didn't get the message.

It's a difficult task for parents to explain every expectation of every person that's under one roof. If that becomes our strategy, the rulebook becomes unwieldy and impractical. Remember our family's rule about dancing in the mall? For Annie, that was a valid regulation, because she found a reason to dance anytime, anyplace. If we had ever caught Matt dancing in public, it was time to bring out the thermometer and children's Tylenol, because he was not well. So the part of our vision that kept each member of our family in check was that we should always be aware of other people and considerate of them. When Annie made that connection, she could understand why her momentary outbursts of joy needed to be redirected. Probably one of the reasons she became a theater teacher was so she could legitimize her desire to dance, as well as choreograph others to do the same.

When we set our vision as our family's foundation, clarity happens both as a result and as an ongoing discipline. First, clear understanding is necessary as you sit down together to create the concept of your vision. Then, as your vision is maturing, that clarity becomes an outgrowth of it. A no-doubt mentality about who your family is and what you stand for is then no longer just an idea but a real part of your personality. There is no longer a need for a long list of dos and don'ts, but rather a simple, straightforward definition of who your family is and who you want to become. Then, as situations arise in your family's life, you have the why already in place. The reason for good behavior is built in to the principles in your vision.

Practice Good Communication

Making clarity a part of your family's DNA calls for a purposeful effort on everyone's part. But mom and dad have to take the lead, and then it's also up to them to keep the ball rolling. In order to build clear communication in our homes, there are some specific practices that are crucial.

Clarity through Conversation

It seems too simple, but the best plan to develop clarity regarding your vision is talking together. Today's culture battles every attempt we make at having real, effective conversation in our homes. Time pressures limit the opportunities we might have, and when we find the chance, everyone in the family seems to be immersed in their own world of video, audio, or digital diversions. "Screen time" is replacing face time in virtually every family. The art of conversation is slipping away from us and with it, the best opportunity to bring clarity to our homes.

Now is your chance to become a superhero. Grab the nearest cape, squeeze into a pair of flattering tights, and—if you feel the need to remain anonymous—find a mask to wear, because you have a job to do. If you choose to accept this challenge, you'll be taking on the task of rescuing conversation from the brink of destruction and nursing it back to health, right there under your own roof.

Since we've already determined that there's probably not a time that is specifically allotted in most homes to discuss things with the family, you'll have to create it. Set aside specific moments for talking together—the whole family or one-on-one. This time isn't meant for confrontational or disciplinary purposes, though there might be some other occasions for that. This is strictly for the purpose of discovering what's going on in everyone's life. Parents set the tone for it by talking openly about what's on their minds, too. Then make sure everyone gets into the flow of this special time. Occasionally, you can make it simply a time for laughs. But definitely make a specific opportunity for discussing things. Be certain to do plenty of talking, and even more listening.

Since we just mentioned it, listening is something else that doesn't happen nearly enough these days. You learn more about what your family's vision really is if you listen closely to what everyone is saying. Your kids reveal so much in casual comments. What questions are they asking? What subject matter seems to be in their heads?

Constructing that arena where conversation can become a priority within your home will enlighten everyone there to the beauty of who your family really is. It will become the greatest tool you have for discovering how God is developing his vision within each and every person and in your entire family.

Clarity through Repetition

Surprises are great, and we all like to experience them from time to time. But when it comes to creating clear understanding, usually it will be repetition that drives a point home. Repetition, as a learning method, can be traced back to the very first historical references about the processes of education. And even today, in a world where technology drives the education process, repetition is still considered one of the most effective tools that teachers can utilize.

There are aspects of your vision that need to be repeated so your family recognizes and remembers them. Teach them your family's vision, who you are and who you're becoming, then teach them again and again. In your lifetime, there have been some classic commercials on television that absolutely grabbed your attention. Creative minds have come up with catchy phrases that stick in your head forever:

"You deserve a break today" (McDonald's).

"It's finger-lickin' good" (Kentucky Fried Chicken).

"Just do it" (Nike).

"Have it your way" (Burger King).

This is your chance to become an advertising mogul by coming up with a clever catchphrase that restates each facet of your vision and makes it memorable. You'll be able to remind everyone what your vision is by simply stating these phrases. It won't be long before everybody in your house will know who your family is and what you represent with your vision. So you shouldn't be surprised if you hear it aimed back at you when you're in some of your weaker moments. You don't have to be offended by it. Just consider yourself successful at getting your message across.

Clarity through Illustration

Understanding abstract ideas is difficult for anyone, especially kids. If you want to effectively teach kids about vision and faith and other intangible concepts that make up your family's identity, you need to become a storyteller. The Bible is a good place to start, since it is full of amazing stories.

Beyond the treasures in Scripture, keep tuned in to other thoughts and ideas that can be developed into creative instruction. Your stories can be funny, serious, mysterious, or heartrending, but they need to get right to the point. Like Aesop and his famous fables, they also need to teach a valuable lesson. This can quickly become a favorite time for your family. It's always something special when your kids can be entertained while they're learning.

Clarity may be the most important of all vision character traits because everything else is dependent on it. Thankfully, you don't have to panic about your role as a parent. There is an amazing promise in the book of James especially for a mom or dad who is determined to instill understanding in their kids' lives. "If you need wisdom, ask our generous God, and he will give it to you. He will not rebuke you for asking. But when you ask him, be sure that your faith is in God alone. Do not waver, for a person with divided loyalty is as unsettled as a wave of the sea that is blown and tossed by the wind" (James 1:5–6).

God honors your determined commitment to your vision by promising you wisdom. When your goal is to bring clarity and understanding into your home, God gives you a special gift of insight, seeing the people and situations in your family through his eyes. His Holy Spirit gives you a sensitivity to determine what each person needs to develop his or her own calling and to join that of your family.

"Let me make this perfectly clear . . ." When you do more than just say it, and really accomplish it, you can be certain that God will honor it. Pause, think, pray, and then allow God to speak clear, comprehensible truth through you into the life of your family.

Focus

Does your family have a vision in place right now? What are the elements?

As you look down the road from where you are now to the realization of your vision, what do you see as the mile markers, or steps, along the way?

What are the roadblocks?

What are the things that God must do?

What are the things that *you* have to do?

The Story Circle

This is an entertaining way to bring out the storyteller in each member of your family. Sit in a circle together, and one person begins to tell a story. There are no limitations to what it can be about, as long as it's tasteful, of course. Whether it's for a few seconds, or on and on for several minutes, when that person feels a need for the next person to continue, he or she simply says, "And then . . . " The next person in the circle picks up where the story left off, making an attempt at being even more creative, more dramatic, or more hilarious. The circle continues in the same way until the story has run its course, and the last person gets to come up with the big conclusion. Everybody in the circle gets at least one chance at every story you begin. It's always a lot of fun, and it stretches each family member's imagination and creativity while making talking together a pleasant experience.

Chapter Nine

Finding Identity through Your Vision

"Kids today are disrespectful, entitled, materialistic, spoiled and self-absorbed—snapping selfies all the time, obsessing about fame and consuming [terrible] music."[1]

—Miami Herald, *February 25, 2014*

"The youth of the world today is touched with madness, literally sick with an aberrant condition of mind."[2]

—Robert Lindner, psychologist, 1954

"Modern youth . . . are selfish and inconsiderate, thinking of no one's comfort or pleasure but their own."[3]

—Chicago Tribune, *May 20, 1928*

"Our youth now love luxury. They have bad manners, contempt for authority; they show disrespect for their elders and love chatter in place of exercise; they no longer rise when elders enter the room; they contradict their parents, chatter before company; gobble up their food and tyrannize their teachers."[4]

—Socrates, poet and philosopher, 390 BC

So this terrible teenager thing that we hear about is nothing new. From the beginning of time, adults haven't been able to figure them out, so they declare that those kids are going to ruin everything. They seem to forget what it was like to be a teenager. Every generation of kids has flustered their elders, leaving them shaking their heads and wondering out loud how these crazy teenagers got into this mess. So far, society has survived, so maybe we should all just take a deep breath and do our very best to keep the lines of communication open. We can be pretty certain that this year's group of terrible teens will mature and come to their senses, just like every one of us has.

Even though this eternal struggle sometimes reveals itself in rebellion and bad behavior, the source of the problem is usually not quite as dark as rampant defiance. When children reach the teen years, they suddenly have the will and the freedom to begin to define just who they are. They are seeking identity and a place to belong. For some who haven't had sufficient foundation and coaching, this search can become more frantic.

The whole process of seeking identity actually starts long before the teen years. The desire to belong to something is within every one of us, from our earliest childhood. Some psychologists label it a "pack mentality." We believe it's not so primal, but instead it's a hunger that God puts within each of us to be in relationship. He created human beings for the purpose of relationship. He is love defined, and his will and desire was to share that love and receive love in return. After he created Adam, he profoundly stated that it wasn't good for man to be alone. God's will was that life was to be shared with others, including himself.

Relationships within a family are crucial in shaping a child's identity. When your family has a clear vision for who they are, then very naturally your kids will begin to identify with it. And as they grow into their teen years, the likelihood that they will need to find that identity somewhere else will diminish. Teens without that family identity just aren't comfortable in their own skin. Peer pressure and cultural icons are loud, so they gravitate to those in order to belong.

If building that identity is so crucial, then we need to find a venue from which we can effectively create an atmosphere for it. You can't preach identity into a kid's heart, and you can't discipline a sense of belonging into them. The most effective way to communicate it is through something very simple—telling a story.

Dr. Elaine Reese is a professor of psychology at the University of Otago in New Zealand. In an article published in *The Atlantic*, she wrote her observations.

> In the preteen years, children whose families collaboratively discuss everyday events and family history more often have higher self-esteem and stronger self-concepts. And adolescents with a stronger knowledge of family history have more robust identities, better coping skills, and lower rates of depression and anxiety. Family storytelling can help a child grow into a teen who feels connected to the important people in her life.[5]

Sharing Family Stories

Knowing your own family stories will enable your children not only to find identity within their own heritage, but it will also help them identify with other people who have stories to tell. Growing up hearing your stories will inevitably allow your kids to become more sensitive to the thoughts and experiences of others.

Jesus knew the value of telling stories to communicate identity with his kingdom. The Scriptures recount almost fifty of his parables that informed, cautioned, encouraged, or enabled his listeners. Jesus's stories made connections with all types of people, making his truth relevant to who they were and what they needed.

So what kinds of stories do we share within our families? What will produce identity with the vision that we're developing within our homes and bring to each person there a personal sense of belonging?

Stories about Our Faith

Your personal narrative about your own spiritual journey may be the greatest gift you can give your family. The beautiful thing about this story is that there's always something new to tell. Our victories, struggles, and questions, our moments of inspiration and realization, or the simple closeness that we feel with our God are all important for our families to share. Your personal faith story will be significant in establishing your family's vision in your children's lives.

Stories about Our Family

What memories do you have of your childhood? What do you know about your family tree? When you tell what it was like when you were a kid, your children will discover that you can really identify with each other. When they come to the realization that you've been in their shoes, they feel more comfortable sharing their thoughts with you. If there have been generations of Christ-followers in your family, introduce stories about them. Even better, if grandparents are around, include them in the actual storytelling.

So that you might get a better idea about family stories and how to make them effective in reaching your children, we thought we would include some of our own. These have become treasures to all of us, and they live on as they're passed from generation to generation.

Greg's Grandma, "Bum-Bum"

My grandmother, a feisty redhead who lived to be a spunky 103, was our guest for dinner one night when our kids were in their early teens. She was the kind of grandma that young people adored, because she always made it a point to ask details about their lives, and she showed a sincere interest in all they had to say and everything they were participating in. But on this night, Annie and Matt turned the tables and began to quiz her for details of what life had been like for her as a teenager.

As she described being a pastor's daughter in a small town in the 1920s, we were all fascinated to hear that she was the first girl in town to get a bob haircut, and that her younger sister followed right behind her. Those two girls were the talk of the town for a few weeks, but the trend caught on, and soon lots of girls were visiting the barber shop.

She described working at a restaurant near the train station and the day that a "railroad man" came in for a meal. He called her "Red" and joked with her. The fun-loving Irishman was very different from her more restrained German family, and he ended up capturing her heart. I had never heard details of that story, and was intrigued to know why my grandfather had been the only person ever to call my grandma "Red," which he did until the day he died.

Her stories allowed our kids to make a new connection with their great-grandmother, and they sought her company, and her prayers and advice, on a regular basis throughout their teen years.

A War Story

(one of Martha's family stories)

My daddy had the Irishman's gift for telling a great story, and I remember clearly one summer afternoon in the late 1950s, when he had his trunk of World War II memorabilia out, going through its contents. He picked up a banged-up tin box that had held chocolates, and he opened it to reveal a red armband with a Nazi swastika, a brown leather billfold, and a silver-toned metal insignia. He explained to me what they were, and he told me the following story.

It was December of 1944. My dad, a twenty-four-year-old American pilot, had just landed a glider behind enemy lines at Bastogne, in the famed Battle of the Bulge.

It had been a dangerous mission, guiding the flimsy aircraft through flak and landing it in a snowy clearing, so that Allied troops who were surrounded and under siege would have the food, medicines, and ammunition that they needed to survive.

But the danger was not over, because now he had to somehow make his way on foot out through enemy lines to join back up with his company. As he was working his way through the woods, he came upon the scene of a previous battle. He discovered the body of a fallen German officer, and taking a great risk, he decided to put on that officer's uniform and use it as a disguise.

"As I took his clothes, this armband, and the hat that had this insignia on it, I was just thinking of him as the enemy," Daddy explained. "But then I found his wallet," he said, showing me that it still contained German Reichsmarks. "When I saw that, it hit me that this was a man, like me. He probably had a wife and kids who would be sad that he had died. And it occurred to me that he might not even have been truly a supporter of what Hitler was doing, but it had come to the point where he had to go along to protect his family, or his own life.

"Let this be a lesson to you, kiddo," Daddy said to me, lightly tapping the wallet as he spoke. "There will be times in your life when you need to speak up for what is right, even though everyone else seems to be going along. If this guy had spoken up at the beginning, others might have joined him, and Hitler might never have come to power.

"It always costs something to stand for what is right," he told me. "But the longer you wait to speak up, the more it is going to cost you."

Daddy walked safely out that day, simply returning the salutes of the German soldiers he passed who thought he was an officer. He was allowed to keep the armband, the insignia, and the wallet as reminders of that day.

Daddy's story for his ten-year-old daughter made a lasting impression, and it has served as a guidepost for me many times over the years.

He died when I was seventeen, so my children never got to know him, but I told them his story more than once as they grew up, showing them the insignia, the shameful armband, and the wallet, which still contains the money that was in it on that day. I often shared the story with my high school journalism students over the years as well.

Today, my seven-year-old grandson knows the story of Grandpa Barney, because his mother has told it to him, and he loves to look at the Air Medal his great-grandfather was awarded as a result of that mission.

Both of my children have passed around the artifacts and told the story to their own high school students, and those kids also seem to take to heart the wisdom found in it.

> I don't think my father ever imagined the far-reaching effect of that little life story he shared with the ten-year-old hanging over his shoulder as he cleaned out his garage.
>
> But that's the power of a story.

Creating Storytime

What do your stories look like?

Age-appropriate

Some stories can be scary or confusing for little ones. Be sure your family shares stories that are appropriate for everyone there. Think before you talk!

Inclusive

Everyone in the family should feel comfortable during story times. They should feel free to express their thoughts, ask questions, or just sit quietly and listen.

Inspiring

Stories that inspire us make a real impact. Though you don't have to avoid stories about difficult things, make sure they end with a redemptive, positive moral.

Nonthreatening

Your story times aren't formal times when everyone is required to sit still and listen quietly. They're simply conversations.

Stories about Our Framework

The best way to communicate your family's vision is to recollect stories that illustrate who God intends your family to be. Discuss times you worked together as a family. Talk about adventures and things you enjoyed together. Then summarize the story by saying, "We are really good at . . . ," or "Our family always reaches out to others."

Telling your stories is an easy way to establish identity among your family members. If at first you're not comfortable sharing so openly, just keep trying, and soon you're sure to feel more relaxed and free. It's such an effective way to communicate the overall vision that God has for you, creating a stable foundation that each member of your family can build on.

"I'm a Pioneer"

(one of Martha's family stories)

When our daughter was young, I enjoyed telling her an exciting tale about my grandfather's ancestors, the Wards, because it had all the elements of a great story.

At the end of the Civil War, the women and children packed up all of their belongings and started out on foot from Fort Smith, Arkansas, across what was Indian Territory in Oklahoma, to meet the men of the family who were setting up for a fresh start in Texas.

The women suffered many setbacks on the journey. The milk cow died. The livestock sickened and died. Weeks into the journey, coming to the end of their provisions, they were able to eat only what one of the women could shoot as they made their way across the empty expanse of eastern Oklahoma Territory. It had been days since they were able to find game, and though they were becoming weak from hunger, they determinedly struggled on.

Just as their strength was failing, they spotted another party coming toward them on the trail. It was the men, who had set out to look for them!

I always ended the adventure by telling Annie, "You come from a line of strong women!"

As a freshman in college, she was required to complete a three-mile run within a certain time period to earn credit for a physical education course. Not coming from a family with a tradition of enjoying unnecessary perspiration or exertion, Annie had spent the whole semester dreading this fitness test.

She started the run on a balmy Saturday morning, but as weather can do in Oklahoma, a cold front blew in. She found herself dressed in shorts and a T-shirt, trying to finish the course against a cold wind carrying sleet and snow, a huge challenge to her native South Texas sensibilities.

Her roommate, who had been an accomplished athlete in high school, was surprised when Annie passed her in the last stretch of the run. As they headed back to the dorm, she asked Annie, "Wow. What got into you? You blew past me and didn't even give me a glance."

"I'm a Ward woman, that's all," Annie told her.

The minute she completed the run, she called to let us know the outcome, describing in full drama-major detail the horror of each little ice pellet. In the middle of her tale of woe, I asked her, "How in the world did you manage to finish like that?"

"I just remembered Poppa's family," she said. "I kept repeating over and over in my head, with every stride, 'I *am* a pioneer, I *am* a pioneer,' until I got to the finish line."

The Apron

(Martha responds to one of Greg's family stories)

It's a faded brown-gingham apron, hand-stitched, trimmed with a ribbon and a row of equally faded pinkish rickrack.

They say she never was without her apron, and sure enough, the photo I have shows her wearing a similar one as she stands beside her husband in a field, looking stoically at the camera in the fashion of her day.

Her life was more difficult than I can fathom.

Her husband was a circuit-riding preacher, and with their eight children, they moved from place to place, wherever he was needed, picking cotton on other people's land and eating and sleeping and living in temporary houses borrowed from other people for the length of their stay.

She was a tiny woman, under five feet tall and weighing about eighty-five pounds, but she dragged the huge sack, weighing more than she did by the time it was full of cotton, behind her as she worked her way up and down the rows in the sun. Singing.

My husband's great-grandmother, Nettie Stiewig, worked hard laboring in the fields, helped educate her children, cooked meals, did laundry, and somehow found time to create some of the most exquisite embroidered and crocheted linens I have ever seen.

But the story of her life, the one thing I really know about her, is that she sang.

Up and down the rows, back bent, fingers raw to the point of bleeding, she worked in the heat and the dust with her husband and children toiling nearby.

But instead of complaining about the work, or wishing she could express her homemaker's artistic heart in a house of her own, Grandma sang joyful, unending hymns to the Savior she loved.

In doing so, she left a legacy that lives still in the hearts of four generations after her.

We've been talking in our Sunday school class about our personal stories and how they are part of God's big, eternal story. We all want to do that One Great Thing for Jesus, and we wonder if, should the opportunity arise, we will recognize it and be up for the challenge. Somctimes I think the One Great Thing may not be that obvious, even to ourselves, as we somehow trudge from day to day, task to task, waiting for "something" to happen.

But when I see that apron, where I have lovingly hung it in my kitchen, I hear the message of her life, still powerful in the heart of a great-granddaughter-in-law who never even met her.

My work, through all the little moments and tasks of life, becomes worship when my heart is full of praise to him.

The apron touches me and fills me with the hope that the memory of my life that will echo through the generations after me will be the same as hers: "She worshipped Jesus while she worked. She sang."

Focus

Begin a search for your family's stories, from your own lives so far and from preceding generations.

Invite grandparents, aunts, and uncles for a meal, and ask them questions that will reveal their stories. While "tell us a story" might intimidate some people, questions like "Tell us about a time God really answered your prayer," or "What was the hardest thing you had to overcome as a teenager?" are easy prompts to get the stories rolling.

Afterward, think and talk about any patterns you discover in God's dealings with your family.

Chapter Ten

Finding Security through Your Vision

What are you afraid of? Before you answer that question, first consider that the fear may be the very thing that would prevent your family from living out an exciting, blossoming vision.

Your vision and your security are connected. In fact, they are permanently a part of each other. What determines the richness and fulfillment of your family's vision, though, is how you define security and what you do to obtain it. If we're building our security and safety in response to our fears, we're completely missing the plan that God intended.

There's a disturbing trend that's happening in homes today. In a survey done by LifeWay Research, 82 percent of the parents polled described themselves as being fearful concerning the safety of their children. But at the same time, 33 percent said they really didn't have a plan for what they wanted to accomplish as parents. Just 9 percent of the moms and dads felt that their kids' relationship with God was the most important part of their growing up.[1]

By studying the results of this LifeWay survey, we can reach some logical conclusions about how most parents view their families' security. In the large majority of homes, parents are fearful that something terrible is going to happen to their kids. One-third of all parents really don't have any plan for where their family is headed. So they certainly haven't figured out how to keep their family secure, but then again, they're pretty sure that God doesn't really have that much to do with it.

We can only assume, then, that these parents' fears are driving their decisions. As they watch the media's sensational coverage of news events, they are influenced to make choices about their families based on an emotional reaction. Their vision is simply finding security, somehow and some way. Where can we hide? How can we insulate ourselves? What would be a safe option for our family, just in case something might happen?

Certainly, this culture has its share of threats to the security of your home and family. But that's not a new thing, even in a nation as sophisticated as the United States. Back in the late 1700s and early 1800s, when families were moving westward across the country, disease, wild animals, and natives who were defending their homeland posed hazards. The Civil War divided the country in the 1860s, and over six hundred thousand men, women, and children were killed. In the late 1800s, about two and a half million American children were full-time laborers, working as much as fourteen hours a day in sweatshops. By the early 1900s, there was little hope for the future because only 6 percent of the children graduated from high school, and one of every three children died of some disease. Even as late as the 1950s, polio, tuberculosis, influenza, measles, diphtheria, and meningitis killed hundreds of thousands of American children. The world has always given us plenty to be afraid of.

In the Psalms, we read of a very different set of priorities and attitudes, the antithesis of fear.

> The LORD is my light and my salvation—
> so why should I be afraid?
> The LORD is my fortress, protecting me from danger,
> so why should I tremble?
> (Ps. 27:1)

In a home where the focus is on building and establishing God's vision, parents lead their families in seeking God rather than in seeking temporary solutions in order to avoid situations. A God-given vision can only be fully effective when he is the source. It's not always easy to trust decisions about your family's security to God, but we are assured that he is the one who actually provides protection and safety for us, not our meaningless attempts at it. If we allow ourselves to be stretched only as far as we're comfortable, we will be missing out on much of what God's vision is for our family. As hard as we might try on our own to protect our home and the people who live there, we can't guarantee that we're going to be guarded from every danger.

We live in a broken, fallen world. Tragedy, disease, and death are a part of that world, and happen in the lives of believers and nonbelievers alike. But the difference is that for Christ-followers, death is not the end, and we have the promise that God will be with us through every difficulty and sorrow. Every situation we encounter can and will be redeemed to God's glory, if we allow it.

All the elements of our family's vision require faith and trust in God's care and love. Is he able to take this family, individually and as a unit, refine the gifts he gave us, and lead us to effectively live out our vision? Does he love us enough to keep us from destruction? Is he big enough to handle anything that might endanger us?

The initial commitment to God's care requires a huge step of faith. But the amazing thing about the way God works in us is that once we've taken that step, he begins to shape within us the very security we need to continue in it. That's because he already placed the attributes within us. We were created to be free from fear and courageous enough to walk down any path he sets before us. The more we trust God, the more he makes his care for us evident.

Paul taught Timothy all about this process. "For God has not given us a spirit of fear and timidity, but of power, love, and self-discipline" (2 Tim. 1:7). From this Scripture's perspective, we can learn every detail that God intended concerning our family's security.

Fear

Fear has never been God's idea. Biblical language experts debate the number of times that "fear not" or "do not be afraid" appear in the Scriptures. Many of them say it's 365, one for every day of the year. Whether or not that's accurate, the number is certainly in the hundreds. It's a convenient figure for us to refer to in a time when it seems that every day we're confronted with new risks. God himself is quoted as telling us not to fear, Jesus said it, and angels were sent from Heaven to proclaim it. Even if God and his angelic emissaries had only said it once, that's enough to make the point.

Almost every dictionary defines fear as a feeling or emotion. Not one of them says that it's a fact, or something concrete. Fear is a feeling that we get when we're not certain about what something is, or what is ahead for us. It is the complete opposite of faith. Fear will keep you and your family from stretching far enough to reach your potential—to live out your vision—if you start making your choices and decisions from that frame of reference.

Timidity

And then there's fear's younger brother, timidity. Even after we've committed to a vision, we excuse ourselves from following through with it because we're timid or shy. Somehow, that doesn't seem as severe as being fearful.

It's like taking a trip to the beach. We know the effort it took to get there would be wasted if we never got in the water because we were afraid. So we timidly take a few steps in, just so we can say we've been there. We miss out on the full effect of being in the ocean, though. Just like that trip to the beach, once you venture out 100 percent into living your family vision, you're never again satisfied with just wading into it only knee-deep. After experiencing the fulfillment of a complete commitment to your vision, you will begin to realize the other characteristics that Paul describes in 2 Timothy 1:7.

Power

Our culture has given us a skewed image of what power really is. Most people imagine someone with an Incredible Hulk type of personality, loud and large, moving into a situation and taking over. If that's what we're thinking will be incorporated into our vision, we will undoubtedly be stepping on a lot of toes instead of influencing lives. Unleashing that kind of power tears things apart instead of building them up.

The power that God gives doesn't wreck anything. Instead, it's a strength that sustains you, and often those around you, through difficult circumstances. It is something that keeps you afloat when everything else around you seems to be going under. A world-class sprinter explodes out of the blocks in a powerful display of strength. In a matter of a few seconds, the race is over. A marathon runner's power is not as evident, as he paces himself through the twenty-six-mile course. You very rarely see a sudden burst of speed or strength, but every muscle, every part of that distance runner's body is burning an amazing amount of energy.

God gives us the capacity to demonstrate an enduring power like that. In the middle of tough situations, we don't need to be fearful. As we follow his course, we know that his strength will sustain us.

Love

Fear and timidity are often evident in our relationships with other people. Fear lashes out, and timidity runs and hides, and neither of those responses is good. We don't want our family to pick up on those bad habits, so when God offers to love others through us, we have an opportunity to demonstrate to everyone under our roof a pure, fearless love. Our vision should include how we purposefully love those in our family as well as those around us.

Whether it's the homeless person on the street corner, the noisy neighbor who keeps everyone awake at night, or the grouchy boss who sometimes makes the job miserable, God gives us a mission to love them. But usually our first reaction is self-preservation. It's easy to find a comfortable mind-set that isolates us from that difficult person. We don't have that option though. We are called to love.

Self-Discipline

Usually, our frame of reference for discussing self-discipline is right after we've stepped on the scale and decided that it's time to go on a diet. It's a life pattern we settle into. We see something that we should change, so we grit our teeth and do the exact opposite of what we've been doing in order to get another result.

In some Bible translations, *self-discipline* is interpreted as "a sound mind." A sound mind thinks the truth. It's not a reflex or something that we have to gut check our way through. It's a change in the way we think about things. Instead of reacting to difficult things, a sound mind thinks them through. The self-discipline God seeks is a thoughtful response. How will this affect my family and me? What steps do I need to take to ensure I'm thinking correctly? How does my decision fit into our family's vision? What does God say about this? Am I reacting or am I responding? Thoughtful response to challenging situations broadens your vision. God may surprise you in the way he gives security and safety to your family as you trust him.

Fighting fear is probably the biggest challenge we face in living out our vision. We've been given wisdom to make the logical decisions about our family's safety. Living fearlessly has nothing to do with living irresponsibly. But the most freeing decision we can make about our lives is to trust God, having faith in him rather than reacting to what might happen. Our challenge is that we live our lives to the fullest and that we become, individually and as a family, everything that God intends for us to become. All this with faith, not fear.

Focus

What do you fear most regarding your family?

What do you think could be the source of that fear?

How do you think the Bible verses used in this chapter apply to your fears?

What actions might you take to overcome fear?

Chapter Eleven

Finding Validity through Your Vision

"Today you are you! That is truer than true! There is no one alive who is you-er than you."

—*Dr. Seuss*, Happy Birthday to You

Who better than Dr. Seuss to show us how important it is for kids to be validated for who they are! That theme is repeated in so many of his books. The creature who is just a bit different from everyone else in the story becomes the hero, because who they are is important and useful in helping others.

One of the primary responsibilities that we have as parents is cultivating within our kids the assurance that they are valuable. They need to know that their appearance, their personality, and their talents make up an individual who is commissioned to change their world and adequate for the calling. Living out our family vision can only happen as the people in our home understand their worth to the family and to the world.

Most families have one—someone who is just a bit different from everyone else living under that roof. It seems like this person's approach to almost everything is unique. When everyone else is thinking one way, this individual is not on the same page. That can be frustrating to parents—they might think that if the one kid would conform, everything else would be beautiful. So they try to discipline the child into conformity. Certainly that one child, like all of us, has moments of rebellion that require some redirection. But we need not only to be aware of those moments, but also to recognize the times when it's simply a situation where they just want to make a statement about who they are.

It's not only okay for one of your family members to be different, but it's a strength that gives your family's vision depth and diversity. As God enlightens you about how he wants to work through your family, he will never exclude someone. There's a place for mom and dad and each child to be a part of the big picture.

Since we began this chapter with wisdom from Dr. Seuss, let's look to another figure from that same genre of speaking to children. Fred Rogers greeted kids every weekday, welcoming them into his neighborhood for a visit. Mr. Rogers understood the platform that he had access to, and he took care to use it to build character and strength in the lives of his young listeners. He was tuned in to the importance of validating kids' self-images. In his book *The World According to Mister Rogers: Important Things to Remember*, he said, "Whether we're a preschooler or a young teen, a graduating college senior or a retired person, we human beings all want to know that we're acceptable, that our being alive somehow makes a difference in the lives of others."[1]

Our kids need to know that we don't expect them to become mini versions of their parents in order to be accepted. They need to understand that, even though they might be different, they are important to each member of their family and to the vision God has for them.

The Boy King

In 1 Samuel 16, we read the story of a little boy who became a shepherd, spending his days watching his father's flocks. He sang a lot and played a harp, and his father, Jesse, probably wished that he would be more attentive to the sheep.

One day, the priest Samuel came to their home, announcing that God had chosen one of the sons of the household to become king. So Jesse brought the first son before the priest. And Samuel was impressed with how sharp and strong the young man was. Most certainly, he thought, this is God's choice. But the Lord stopped Samuel and spoke to him. "Don't judge by his appearance or height, for I have rejected him. The LORD doesn't see things the way you see them. People judge by outward appearance, but the LORD looks at the heart" (v. 7). And as Jesse brought his other sons in to meet Samuel, they weren't exactly who God wanted, either.

David, the young shepherd, wasn't as impressive as his older brothers at first glance. Initially, his dad overlooked him in the presentation of his sons because he was different. It wasn't until Samuel asked if there was anybody else that Jesse brought David in from the fields. We can imagine that Jesse might have tried to prepare the priest prior to David's arrival. He may have told him that David might be a bit dirty and smelly because he had been in the fields all day. Or he may have explained that the boy was an artsy type, a musician and a poet, so he wasn't as athletic looking as the other boys in the family.

But when David stood before him, Samuel immediately knew that despite what he looked like or what his resume had to say, young David was who God had chosen to be the King of Israel. Samuel's anointing of David as the future king was the validation that the boy needed to give him the confidence to truly become "a man after God's heart." He wrote his own biography, in reflective worship in the book of Psalms.

> Oh yes, you shaped me first inside, then out;
> you formed me in my mother's womb.
> I thank you, High God—you're breathtaking!
> Body and soul, I am marvelously made!
> I worship in adoration—what a creation!
> You know me inside and out,
> you know every bone in my body;
> You know exactly how I was made, bit by bit,
> how I was sculpted from nothing into something.
> Like an open book, you watched me grow from
> conception to birth;
> all the stages of my life were spread out before you,
> The days of my life all prepared
> before I'd even lived one day.
> (Ps. 139:13–16 *The Message*)

God knows who the people in your family really are, because he's the One who created them. He gifted them to fulfill their calling and to be a part of the vision he's given your family. Their personality, their mannerisms, their thoughts, and their ideas are God's investments in their lives. And, of all the places in this world, home is where those expressions should not only be allowed but encouraged.

As you acknowledge the importance of the people in your home, and when validating their gifting becomes your priority, your vision thrives. You provide a fertile soil for all those things to grow and mature, and your vision expands and extends. Because they find validation and acceptance at home, the members of your family respond with confidence and learn to value and appreciate each person their lives touch.

A Page from the Manning Family Playbook

They've been declared "The First Family of Football," and the Mannings' iconic gridiron performances strengthen their reign as every year passes.

Archie, the patriarch, had fourteen successful seasons as an NFL quarterback, but his career never reached the level that his sons' have. Quarterback Peyton Manning is a five-time NFL Most Valuable Player, and he led both the Indianapolis Colts and the Denver Broncos to Super Bowl championships. Eli Manning quarterbacked the New York Giants to two Super Bowl championships.

There is another Manning brother most people haven't heard of. Cooper Manning is Archie's oldest son. From the beginning, he didn't have his dad's intensity, nor his desire to be a quarterback. He was a very good wide receiver in high school and won a scholarship to his dad's alma mater, the University of Mississippi. Before he could play college football, doctors discovered that Cooper had a degenerative spinal disease, and his football career was ended. He courageously dealt with disappointment, and he has become successful in business.

Every royal family must have a queen on the throne, and the Mannings have Olivia. Archie met her when they were both students at the University of Mississippi. In *The*

Book of Manning, a documentary about the family produced by ESPN, Archie revealed how he fell in love with her. "We just had a lot in common," he said. "Both of us from small Mississippi towns. And I thought she was beautiful. I just felt comfortable."[1]

Olivia has an opinion as to why Archie felt comfortable being around her. "We met at a fraternity-sorority mixer," she said. "We danced, we talked. And I could talk football."

Archie loved football. In fact, it was his life. His passion for the sport started early in his life, when he discovered it was how he could connect with his father, Buddy Manning. "My dad was a football fan, and we would watch football together. He didn't hug. He was a tough guy." So by playing football, Archie got acceptance and attention from him.

"My dad loved Ole Miss football. So that became my dream—to be an Ole Miss quarterback."

When he was offered a scholarship to attend Mississippi, he felt that he had earned his father's approval. In his first season of varsity football for the Rebels, Archie's performance earned him a place in the college football spotlight. Everyone began to predict that he was destined for All-American status.

But one day the following summer, Archie walked into his home and found his dad's lifeless body there. Buddy Manning had taken his own life. "My dad had some stress because his business wasn't good. I never got angry about it. I just accredited it to bad health and a weak time in his faith. I think he was just at a low point in his life." It was one of those situations that really couldn't be explained or justified.

Just weeks later, Archie returned to Ole Miss, determined to deal with it day by day. The tragedy shaped who he was as a man and as a father. "We were so grateful and so blessed to have these kids," Archie said. From the time the boys were barely more than toddlers, he took them everywhere with him. When you quarterback a pro football team, most of your time is spent on the field. So the Manning kids became fixtures at New Orleans Saints' practices. As Archie worked out on the field, the boys had their own football games happening on the sidelines. "I wasn't trying to expose them to it," he said. "I just wanted to spend time with my kids." Whenever they were at home, the Mannings were often in the backyard together, usually playing football. Coaching duties in those backyard games, though, were Olivia's responsibility, while Archie captured the whole thing with his video camera.

The vision Archie and Olivia Manning had for their family was much more than creating quarterbacks. What Archie had missed from his own father, he wanted to make certain to give to his own sons. "I wanted to hug them, and I wanted to tell them I loved them."

"He never really brought football home," Olivia said of her husband. "He would just come home and be dad." The first priority of the Manning household was love and acceptance. Because Cooper, Peyton, and Eli were so close to their father and spent so much time with him, football just rubbed off on them.

The Mannings' vision now extends far beyond their New Orleans home. In 1996, Archie began the Manning Passing Academy in order to work with high school kids not only on football but also on life skills. Over 1,200 campers attend every summer. Peyton and Eli join their dad in teaching quarterbacking skills to the teenagers at the camps. But Archie Manning wanted to include all his sons. Cooper's marketing skills and lively personality have been invaluable in his position as the senior associate director at the camp. Every summer, while Peyton and Eli are on the field teaching passing skills, Cooper can be found leading sessions in the classroom, preparing kids for college life.

For all their success on the football field, Peyton and Eli weren't raised to be quarterbacks. In *The Book of Manning*, Archie recalls a conversation he had with his own father as he was driving him to the University of Mississippi for the first time. "I asked him, 'What do you think I ought to study?' He said, 'Find something you'll be good at. I just want you to be a good guy.' That's what I wanted to be with my children. I hope they think I'm a good guy."

Focus

List each child in your household.

For each person on that list, think about what truly captures his or her interest. What does she like to play, or play with? What kinds of books or movies does he respond positively to?

List what is valuable to your family, and to others, about each one (think beyond talents like athletics or winning karaoke contests, and consider things like good listener, always willing to help, etc.).

It could be fun to designate a day for each person (other than a birthday) and celebrate that child's role in your family.

Chapter Twelve

Finding Integrity Through Your Vision

"Because I said so, that's why!" We never wanted to be *those* parents, and we're sure you didn't want to, either. But, inevitably, those moments came when, out of pure frustration, we couldn't come up with any other logical answer. We consoled ourselves by concluding that, after all, we *were* the mom and dad, and we knew more than the kids did. We never have forgotten, though, the heated moment that one of us (whose identity will remain confidential) actually said to our eight-year-old daughter, "Why don't you just grow up!" *Uhhh, Dad, I think that's what she's doing.*

Even if it's true that "because I said so" is a factual reason, it's an empty statement that teaches our kids nothing. Our daughter, at age eight, was maturing and processing information, but she had a lot to learn about life before she became an adult and could make grown-up decisions. We're happy to say that everything worked out well with her. She is now a very capable young woman who, along with her husband, is doing a wonderful job raising our grandsons.

We have overheard her, though, falling back into her childhood recollections and saying to her boys, "Because I said so."

Kids always seem to want to know why something is the way it is. And the number of times they can ask that question is certainly far beyond every parent's ability to answer it. What if there were some internal switch we could activate that would automatically make every child understand the reasons some things are right and some things are wrong. As far as we know, it hasn't been invented yet, but we can recommend something that might give your whole family a new point of view.

Building a Family of Integrity

Integrity has been defined as doing the right thing even when nobody else is looking. It's the kind of behavior pattern we hope will become part of our children's character. Integrity shapes our vision, and our vision develops our integrity. When our family's integrity is emphasized as an important part of our vision, many times we can actually come close to providing a real answer to the why question.

When our vision and our integrity are combined, they nourish each other within each family member's life. This full circle enables everyone to enjoy a greater measure of peacefulness and harmony, even within challenging circumstances.

Teaching Integrity

Our one-year-old grandson is learning no-no right now. At this point in his life, there are very few things he's been able to get into that required a reprimand, but he's learning new tricks every day. The latest happens when his parents (or grandparents) have him "safely" placed in his playpen. This budding engineer has learned to stack his toys and climb on them, and on a few occasions, he's almost escaped. When he's told "No-no!" he looks up with a rather shocked expression on his face. "You couldn't mean *me*, could you?" It's as if he can't imagine there could be anything wrong with this sophisticated construction project he's working on.

Toddlers aren't the only ones who don't enjoy being corrected. Even when we're thirty, or fifty, or seventy, we don't like to be told no. But self-control and integrity have to be learned, so we address it early and then often after that. One-year-olds have to learn the concept first and then, as they grow and learn to communicate, we teach them in a continual progression more and more details about the philosophy of no-no. When we present the principles of integrity and right behavior, we answer the why for them in advance. Waiting to deal with every questionable motive and action as they happen won't create an understanding of integrity. It will only produce a list of nos that will get longer and longer as the years go by. Sadly, we see many adults who are operating only from that extended list. Their lives are a constant stream of mishaps, brought on by their decisions that have been based on what they can get away with. They never learn the philosophies and ideals that make up good conduct.

In a confrontation with someone in your family, you may make your point, but you rarely are able to answer questions. And when you don't present real answers, nothing is accomplished or learned that makes the child embrace the positive behavior. In a setting apart from the correction and discipline, parents need to discuss the way that bad behaviors disappoint each other and God. Integrity, then, becomes part of your family's vision when you talk about the behavior that's expected of each member of the household, even before there is an issue.

The Pharisees tried to corner Jesus when they questioned him about these issues. He answered with the principles of behavior that are guidelines for us for our entire lives. "'You must love the Lord your God with all your heart, all your soul, and all your mind.'

This is the first and greatest commandment. A second is equally important: 'Love your neighbor as yourself.' The entire law and all the demands of the prophets are based on these two commandments" (Matt. 22:37–40).

General discussions about who your family is, what you stand for, and what your faith is all about can and should involve everyone. This is a great place to begin. Casually and peacefully, without accusing or pointing fingers, emphasize who you are as a family and what constructs your character. As the conversation progresses, you will find opportunities to include why you think that way and why it's important in your home.

Teach your family that God has a plan and a mission for who you are. Every bad decision that's made in your home delays the beauty of what your family can be. Accentuate the dos more than the don'ts, and remind each other about the beauty and potential that live under your roof.

Accepting Integrity

Teaching is effective only if someone listens and learns. Our goal is to get our family not only to hear our principles of behavior but also to understand them and embrace them as their own.

Make it a point to listen to each family member. Some of the more compliant kids will accept your code of conduct, and they will cooperate fully. But there are also those strong-willed ones who will question and challenge. Without giving ground, listen to them and try to help them understand the why of your family's vision. You might find it surprising, too, if they have a valid point that will require you to rethink and adjust your rules. In our family, we understood that those moments weren't a loss for us but instead a big victory. We don't want to name any names within the Singleton family, but even the most stubborn kids, and the adults too, have a hard time disobeying rules that they had a hand in establishing.

Your vision, as well as your rules, may have to be altered somewhat as your kids get older. Don't panic, and certainly don't count it as a setback. An 8:00 P.M. bedtime works for a kindergartner, but not a teenager, and changes like this have to happen as your children mature. Changing the rules is a natural part of the process involved in bringing integrity into our homes.

Rules are important. But they don't always need to cause angry outbursts or in-your-face rebellion. As the members of your family accept what constitutes good behavior, they will begin to see rules as a place of safety for them and a description of your family's character. Once again, though, it requires really listening to what our family members have to say and how they're feeling about themselves and their sense of acceptance and belonging.

Restoring Integrity

Everyone makes mistakes, and we all even willfully disobey at times. When it happens in your home, how it's handled is crucial to maintaining your vision. We can be thankful for the grace that God extends to us all. It's difficult to comprehend how completely he forgives us, and how his love never gives up on us. And he calls for us to demonstrate that same grace to others. "Since God chose you to be the holy people he loves, you must clothe yourselves with tenderhearted mercy, kindness, humility, gentleness, and patience. Make allowance for each other's faults, and forgive anyone who offends you. Remember, the Lord forgave you, so you must forgive others" (Col. 3:12–13).

When someone is disobedient, whether it be a child or a parent, the entire family feels the effect of it. When a family member is outwardly rebellious, we tend to take it personally. Maybe it's because our feelings are hurt, but we often try to protect ourselves by shutting the person out or trying to make sure he or she hurts as much as we did. But God doesn't give us that option. We're expected to extend his grace, and that's actually part of the integrity that he wants to build within our vision. Correction and consequences are part of the discipline process, but forgiveness and compassion are, too.

Remember Jesus's story about the prodigal son? It's found in Luke 15, and it gives a beautiful picture of God's grace and forgiveness extended to us. The young man's father didn't rebuke him or turn him away. In fact, he saw his son far down the road, making his way home. And immediately the father ran to meet him. Just as that dad did, we should be eager to demonstrate grace in our home.

Becoming people of integrity is an important aspect of our vision. It's through our family's integrity that we learn that it's safe to depend on each other and that honesty, even in the face of failure, is always the best course of action. The world sees integrity through your window, and they know that they can count on you. You become the ones others can confide in and the ones who will give them wise counsel. In Romans, Paul painted a beautiful picture of integrity for us to emulate.

> Don't just pretend to love others. Really love them. Hate what is wrong. Hold tightly to what is good. Love each other with genuine affection, and take delight in honoring each other. Never be lazy, but work hard and serve the Lord enthusiastically. Rejoice in our confident hope. Be patient in trouble, and keep on praying. When God's people are in need, be ready to help them. Always be eager to practice hospitality.
>
> Bless those who persecute you. Don't curse them; pray that God will bless them. Be happy with those who are happy, and weep with those who weep. Live in harmony with each other. Don't be too proud to enjoy the

company of ordinary people. And don't think you know it all!

Never pay back evil with more evil. Do things in such a way that everyone can see you are honorable. Do all that you can to live in peace with everyone.

Dear friends, never take revenge. Leave that to the righteous anger of God. For the Scriptures say, "I will take revenge; I will pay them back," says the LORD.

Instead, "If your enemies are hungry, feed them. If they are thirsty, give them something to drink. In doing this, you will heap burning coals of shame on their heads."

Don't let evil conquer you, but conquer evil by doing good. (Rom. 12:9–21)

Focus

List the basic rules that make up the operational integrity of your family. (For example, in most families those would include never lying or stealing, being kind to everyone, etc.) As a family, talk about why those are your rules.

A good way to examine family rules without making it a preaching session could be to read literature or watch a movie together where people are in situations where they are tempted to break rules, or where they do go against the guidelines for living with integrity, and discuss the outcomes for the people in the story.

When our kids were in middle school and early high school, MTV's *The Real World* was a popular reality show. We made it a point to watch with them and then talk about the way the characters handled the situations they found themselves in. We could ask questions like "Why do you think he did that?" or "What do you think is going to happen to her now?" Especially important were "What would you do in that situation?" and, most of all, "What do you think Jesus would want you to do if you were there now?"

The points are better made when it is an impersonal discussion about a scenario than when it is just parents imposing rules, without working to help children understand and own them!

Part Three

Looking Out Your Window

Chapter Thirteen

Your Family's View of Their World

During the time we were writing this book, we took a few days off and made our way to the Texas Gulf Coast. We understand why folks in Florida or California or North Carolina would snicker at that, because we've been to your beaches, and you win. But when you live in San Antonio, and you need a place to get a quick shot of refreshment and inspiration, Padre Island gets the job done. We've cleverly convinced ourselves that it's necessary sometimes when you're writers.

Our bedroom at the condo had a huge sliding glass door that opened up on to a second-floor balcony overlooking the Gulf of Mexico. So every morning, we woke to a beautiful sunrise over the water. The colors in the sky, the sparkle on the blue waves, reminded us of the beauty of all of God's creation. It was breathtaking.

Had we kept the drapes drawn and never looked out that window, we would have missed a grand display of God's creativity. If we had let ourselves become distracted by something else, we never would have experienced the joy that the beautiful view gave us. We would have missed out on one thing that provided so much of the refreshment and inspiration we soaked up that weekend.

When God creates a vision for us in our home, it's not just so others can watch us, pat us on the back, and assure us of what a great job we're doing of being a family. He never replaces that window with a one-way mirror so we can't see out. He wants us to have a clear view of everything going on outside our house, and he has a distinct purpose for doing that. The most important part of the vision he gives us is that, when we view the world, we walk outside our doors and share his love.

The worldview we embrace inside our home is crucial to discovering and fulfilling the vision that God has for our family. So it's very important that we determine what he has in mind. How important is the rest of the world in God's eyes? He loves it so much that he gave his Son to die for it. In today's Christian culture, we sometimes hear too much about separating ourselves from the world and being apart from it. It's an attitude that some say is endorsed by Scripture. But it's very important that we understand exactly what it means to be set apart, so we can accomplish what God wants to do in us and through us, individually and as a family.

What was important to Jesus? What was such a priority for him that he would make it a matter for discussion with his Father? In John 17, we're given the opportunity to listen in on Jesus's prayer.

> Now I am coming to you. I told them many things while I was with them in this world so they would be filled with my joy. I have given them your word. And the world hates them because they do not belong to the world, just as I do not belong to the world. I'm not asking you to take them out of the world, but to keep them safe from the evil one. They do not belong to this

> world any more than I do. Make them holy by your truth; teach them your word, which is truth. Just as you sent me into the world, I am sending them into the world. And I give myself as a holy sacrifice for them so they can be made holy by your truth. (John 17:13–19)

Within this prayer, Jesus reveals some priorities about how he and his Father view the world, and how he wants his followers to relate to their world around them. He provides for us some specific directions about the attitudes that he wants us to instill in our families, too.

Our Family Is Different

Jesus makes it very clear that our citizenship is not in this world, but in the kingdom of God. We are aliens, and yet the planet Earth is where we reside. We shouldn't expect our family to be like everyone else. We won't always fit in with all the other families. So our goal is to be active participants in this world without conforming to the culture. We teach our kids and remind each other that there will be times we'll just be different, and sometimes it might be uncomfortable, or it could even hurt a bit. But being different will be the very thing that makes us who we were created to be as a family.

Facing the "Now What?" Moments

After you've made the decision to live out God's vision for your family, there will inevitably be moments and events that cause you to ask, now what?

Sometimes, as we try to rationally reason things out, it can get a bit scary. We might find ourselves in places that are uncomfortable. But once we determine that our circumstances are God designed, we need to take the risk and move on confidently.

A while back, we spoke at a MOPS (Mothers of Preschoolers) meeting about discovering your family's vision. At the conclusion, one of the moms, Sarah, came up to us and asked us to pray for her family. She told us they were moving to Egypt on an extended mission trip. And even though she was confident that it was God's idea and part of his vision for their family, she was becoming fearful about all the things that could happen while they were there.

We were intrigued by this family's bold steps. So we asked her if she could send us an email, giving us some further details about their move. A few weeks later, we received this message from her.

Hello Greg & Martha!

When you came to speak at our MOPS meeting last month you asked me to email you about our decision to move our family to Egypt. I'm sorry it has taken me a month to do it. As you might be able to imagine, life is a bit hectic for me right now.

We are moving to Egypt with an architectural ministry (my husband is an architect). We will arrive the beginning of February for a minimum of three years. We have a 2½-year-old daughter and 8-month-old son. And we can only take what we can get on the plane with us. Whew!

How did we get to this decision? Six years ago my husband found this ministry and we applied for a semester internship with them in Guatemala for the semester after we graduated from college. We got to experience living cross-culturally and working with the ministry and decided it was something we would like to do more full-time in the future.

We came back to the States to do graduate work (he in architecture and me in counseling). Three years ago we took a short trip to Egypt to scout with a team where they might put the next office. We got excited about being a part of this new office, learning Arabic, living in Egypt, using our skills and gifts in this way. So for three years we have been waiting on the right timing.

In many ways this doesn't seem like perfect timing. Our kids are very young and we'd like to still have more. We are still young (not even 30 yet!) and Josh could use more experience professionally. But as we talked with the director of the office in Egypt and the human resources director here in the States, we saw how God was putting it all together. The office needs an architect (the three staff there are engineers). We are willing and wanting to go.

Sometimes I question the timing. Sometimes I think it would be better if the kids were older so that they could have better relationships with their grandparents. It would be better if we were finished having babies so I don't have to figure out where to deliver. It would be better if . . .

But what we keep coming back to is that God has put this all together. He has provided for everything. One of the requirements for going on staff is raising our own salary and moving expenses. God has done that for us in six months! All while my husband was working full-time and we had a toddler and newborn. That is a miracle in itself. He has put together this team we will be joining that is excited for us to come, is praying for us, and that we feel a part of already.

I don't know that there is an ideal time. We have to trust and be obedient to what God asks of us. We are excited to see what He is going to do in this next season. Right now I am overwhelmed with what needs to happen for us to get on that plane. We are trusting that He will provide for, protect, and continue to sanctify us through this time.

It's not a decision we came to lightly but in some ways it was a simple decision. It's the following through on that decision that is the harder part. =)

Sincerely,
Sarah

In the process of discovering God's vision for your family, you may face things that make you uncomfortable. You must remember, though, that uncomfortable isn't always a bad thing. God made it very clear that none of our decisions should be made on a basis of fearing what might happen. It's through difficult and uncertain situations like this that God stretches us and expands our opportunities as a family. If you're facing those moments now, surround yourselves with people who will pray for you and give you thoughtful, wise counsel. Be strong!

Update!

We received the following email from Sarah while we were writing this book. In her blog, she shares the struggles and the victories in their family's adventure of faith.

> Hello Greg & Martha,
>
> How thoughtful of you to think of me! Yes the trip did work out. My husband and kids and I have been living in Egypt for the past 4 years. We've had quite a few adventures and many opportunities to share grace with those around us. Parenting and marriage relationships are big issues here as there is such a limited amount of resources and solid helpful information. My husband is an architect working for a small design firm and he has gotten to work on some very interesting projects, particularly hospitals with doctors who aim to treat the body and the heart.
>
> Thanks again for saying hello and remembering me. I hope all is well with your family.
>
> Here is our blog if you want to read about our adventures: walkegyptian.wordpress.com.
>
> Warmly,
> Sarah

Our Family Doesn't Have to Be Fearful

We have bad news and good news. The bad news is that there is no possible way parents can protect their kids from every threat—physical, mental, emotional, and spiritual—that confronts us in this world. We have an enemy, and the Bible tells us that he exists to "steal, kill, and destroy." That would be scary enough to make us board up the windows and never step out of our homes, except for one thing. God the Almighty, our Father, tells us that he is protecting us, so we don't have anything to worry about. That's the good news. Fear for our family's well-being comes when we decide it's our responsibility to protect them. God never asks that of us, because he's the one who has our back.

That doesn't mean we should be like a guy with vertigo who decides to become a tightrope walker. But it does mean that people, situations, circumstances, and tasks don't ever need to intimidate us. We should never use fear as a factor in making decisions for our family. It will always limit the adventure of living out the vision that God has for our family. Every time, fear will interfere with fulfillment.

Our Family Has a Calling

In Matthew 5, Jesus specifically describes who we are as Christ-followers. We are called to be salt and light on this planet. And, just as individual disciples were given this responsibility, our family's vision is formed in response to it. Salt and light are two elements that immediately change the environment to which they're added. That's exactly what our family is called to do, too.

As we look out our window and out to our world, everyone in our home must understand that the people there desperately need a demonstration of God's love. We do that by simply living our lives as we're led by his vision for us. Our world doesn't have to be overwhelmed by the saltiness or blinded by the light. They simply need to taste and see the beauty of a life that follows Christ.

God Is at Work in Our Family

Family life, just like the lives of every individual, is always changing. Wherever God places our family, we will be surrounded by faces of those who need him. That circle may broaden or diminish, or it might drastically change because of circumstances in which we find ourselves, but God is always at work to prepare us to fulfill the calling. He's given us his Word, which we must depend on to strengthen our home. And he's given us each other, to provide love, support, encouragement, and acceptance for one another. As each day unfolds, we need to remind each other of God's commitment to us and our commitment to one another. That kind of atmosphere under our roof allows God a free hand to work in us as a family. And that's how we're able to fulfill our vision and our mission.

Every day, open that window wide, and allow everyone in your family to see the world that God loves so much. Take on your calling confidently, knowing that God has equipped your family to become exactly who he desires that you are. Let your home be the place that houses the people who enable and encourage everyone there to boldly become everything they are called to be. Let it be the place that is open to those who need love, grace, comfort, and peace. God doesn't call us to a world outside our window that will be safe and easy. But he promises that, with him, our families can experience a rich, fulfilling reality that changes our lives and the lives of everyone around us.

Focus

Where have you travelled?

What moved you or inspired you about the different places you have visited, or people you have met?

If you have done brief mission trips, either as a youth or as an adult, what were the challenges of the experiences? What were the benefits?

Does your church or denomination sponsor missionaries? How much do you know about these people and the work they do?

Are you aware of any needs in the places, or of the missionaries and their families, that your family might be able to supply?

A great family activity that can open your kids' eyes to what it looks like to impact the world beyond the neighborhood would be to read together books like *Through Gates of Splendor*, by Elisabeth Elliot, or *Bonhoeffer Student Edition: Pastor, Martyr, Prophet, Spy*, by Eric Metaxas. There is also a movie based on Elliot's book, called *End of the Spear*, that you could watch if reading won't work at your house.

Chapter Fourteen

Having an Others-Centered Vision

"Let me give you a new command: Love one another.
In the same way I loved you, you love one another.
This is how everyone will recognize that you are my disciples—
when they see the love you have for each other."

—*John 13:34–35*, The Message

Jesus opened up an entirely new perspective to our vision with these verses in John 13. The Bible is so full of references to loving one another that, sadly, we might sometimes forget the impact of his love at work in our world. Love may be the least difficult theme in our faith to explain or comprehend, so we tend to overlook the power it contains. We could discuss just who it is we should love, or how we should make it known to them. But it's clear that loving others is not just a suggestion, it's a command.

As each family's vision begins to unfold, certainly the personalities and talents represented in that home will make their vision unique. But there's one thing that all of us have in common—our vision's foundation is an others-centered proposition. It's never about how we look, or what we accomplish, but it's about the needs of the people in the world around us.

Jesus had even more to say about this in the book of Matthew.

> Then the King will say to those on his right, "Enter, you who are blessed by my Father! Take what's coming to you in this kingdom. It's been ready for you since the world's foundation. And here's why:
>
> I was hungry and you fed me,
> I was thirsty and you gave me a drink,
> I was homeless and you gave me a room,
> I was shivering and you gave me clothes,
> I was sick and you stopped to visit,
> I was in prison and you came to me."
>
> Then those "sheep" are going to say, "Master, what are you talking about? When did we ever see you hungry and feed you, thirsty and give you a drink? And when did we ever see you sick or in prison and come to you?" Then the King will say, "I'm telling the solemn truth: Whenever you did one of these things to someone overlooked or ignored, that was me—you did it to me." (Matt. 25:34–40 *The Message*)

The philosophy of what Jesus was telling us is unquestionable. Loving and serving others is a universal calling for every believer and every family. Within the framework of each individual's and each family's vision, though, the process might look very different. For every unique personality, there is a facet of service that

God has before us. We wanted our friends to take it from here, to inspire you and motivate you to discover the places and the people you will reach out to. So we just asked them on Facebook to share what their family had done together, and what they thought was a great way to serve others. Now you get to look over our shoulders to see what some of them had to say.

> CONNIE: Food bank
>
> AMBER: We collect change all year in a piggy bank then Christmas Eve wrap it up and deliver it to a family in need. (Usually by knocking and driving off). Usually by the end of the year, there's a lot of cash in there and we always contribute some nice size bills on top.
>
> REBECCA: Children's Hunger Fund Toy Wrap (gifts are sent around the world); Christian Assistance Ministry (local); Soldiers' Angels (local organization, but reaching the far ends of the earth). All are family friendly. IF your family wants to do something on your own, you can do a sock drive (Stevie organized one at her school and we sent them to soldiers and handed them out to the homeless, or a diaper drive (work with local companies for collection sites); host an event at a nursing home (I've always wanted to do a '50s sock hop!); or you can just stand on the side of the street and give out hugs . . . I've NEVER passed up a free hug!!! LOL!
>
> DESTINEE: In high school I volunteered at the food bank sometimes and always saw families volunteering together! As for around the world, do you remember the Style Your Sole days we did with Toms Shoes? Maybe you could set one up in your community or at your church!

TRACEY: We sponsor a child in another country as a family. He writes the family letters twice a year and we write back. He is the same age as our son and we have been a sponsor since he was about 4.

Other ideas: food bank, visits to a nursing home, canned goods drive, neighborhood/community beautifying projects, pet shelters, places like Boysville or St PJs welcome entire families to volunteer. Christmas boxes are coming up. The shoebox movement.

I think now more than ever you could talk with a family about refugees, and Red Cross would be a good resource for the global perspective.

GLENANNE: Volunteer at a neighborhood food pantry. Pack gallon size Ziploc bags with food, socks and toiletries, and pass out to people you see on the street.

As for serving globally, look for a feed-starving-children packing event in San Antonio. It's a great way for an entire family to serve together.

DENNIS: How about Elf Louise?

JANA: Invite other families over for dinner. Teach the kids about generosity with money.

JON: Bring them here to Rosarito, Mexico, to build a house on one weekend for a family that desperately needs one!

PAMELA: Globally: raise money for water wells. Heifer Fund to buy livestock. Locally . . . Take small items to a nursing home . . . Toiletries. Sing and play games with the residents . . . Goody bags for the homeless with socks, toiletries, water bottles, crackers, snacks . . . Invite foreign students from a local college to join in a meal.

FRED: There is a great organization here in Waco called World Hunger Relief. They do this here and internationally. http://worldhungerrelief.org/

EARLEEN: Take Saturday to spend at a local agency like Salvation Army and volunteer. One Thanksgiving we went to a homeless mission and served Thanksgiving dinner to those in need. It blessed us beyond measure.

BELINDA: Get totes or purses from thrift stores or donations. Fill with toiletries and pass out to homeless women.

SHER: Servers for Thanksgiving dinner at a shelter. We have gospel missions, Tarrant County food banks, Mission Arlington. Sponsor for Compassion International or Samaritan's Purse.

DONNIE: When our children were younger, and we lived in Midland, Texas, we all participated for several years in a project called Christmas in April helping low income families with home repairs from something as little as painting rooms to something larger such as putting on new roofs, and other types of repairs. Several times during the Christmas holidays when we lived in Midland, my wife Peggy took the kids and helped pack and deliver food boxes from the Baptist Crisis Center to needy families. Another idea is if you know someone who has recently had a death in the family you could take food to them and get their shoes and shine them so they will look nice for the funeral. Doing things like this will be a blessing to your family.

CINDY: Deliver Meals on Wheels

CAROLINA: Haven for Hope needs people to help serve and clean up after meals.

MARGIE: Help the elderly and the widows and widowers by getting groceries, cleaning, or just visiting with them. The elderly love children and young people, and like to tell stories of the past. Some like to sing so you could sing some of their favorite hymns or songs. We can all learn a lot from the elderly.

MARILYN: Volunteer on ongoing basis at a nursing home or assisted living, doing activities with the residents. Get to know them and let them, above all, "tell their story."

One time things such as Smile of a Child Shoebox—let them shop. Physical jobs with elderly neighbors, church groups, Habitat, etc. Backyard Bible School in the summer—great fun. Let them know when you are making a monetary contribution to an organization—how and why you have chosen the group.

BERS: Presbyterian Disaster Assistance (you can help from home), Buckner International (they can take groups) are just a few!

You can also help at Catholic Worker House; they are there every day and you can help with breakfast and lunch. They always love people helping out!

CAROL: Delivering Thanksgiving dinners to families through an organization in Arlington, Texas. Welcomed home the soldiers at the airport when they were arriving back in the states for R&R. Volunteering at the local animal shelter. Shopping for Salvation Army Angels.

ROBBIE: Fix up a yard in the neighborhood. Cutting the grass. Weed eating. Pick up shavings. Trim trees. Edge. Etc. But have everyone participate. Then the family writes a message on a card and leaves it at the door.

So, there are some suggestions from some of our friends for ways to start serving. You can also ask your pastor about foreign or local missions that your church supports and how your family might be a part of it. Do an Internet search of the service organizations in your city. Some of them welcome families who want to help, but if they don't, they probably can refer you to someone who does. Communities in Schools is a national organization that gives assistance to at-risk students and their families in virtually every part of the country. Visit with them in your local public schools and let them show you how you can help.

What your family will learn through serving is life-changing. Not only do you discover the joy that comes through giving, but with each experience, you'll sense a growing hunger to serve even more. May God bless your family as you set out on your mission!

Focus

What opportunities does your church offer to serve your community?

What needs do you see?

What organizations are in place in your community that could use help from your family? For example, many cities have an active Habitat for Humanity program, or a food bank, that welcomes volunteers.

Is there a nursing home near you that needs something your family can offer?

From the list you make, find something that your family can all do together, and make it a point to participate within the next month or two.

Chapter Fifteen

When Vision Becomes Mission

In December 1969, the United States was embroiled in a bloody war in Vietnam. Almost twelve thousand American soldiers had been killed just during that year, many of them under twenty-one years old. And there seemed to be no end of the conflict in sight. The college culture answered with nonconformity and rebellion. Their reasoning was that they wanted to be nothing like the authority figures that had brought the country to this situation. "Don't trust anyone over thirty," they warned each other. And their new mantra was, "If it feels good, do it." So drug use, promiscuous sex, and many other antiestablishment activities prevailed. It was a "me first" atmosphere, with many of the students trying to drown out the horror of war and death with any manner of self-gratification.

Louise Locker was a twenty-year-old sociology major at Trinity University in San Antonio. She was trying to find herself, like most other students throughout the United States, on a journey of discovering who she was to become. One evening, she was watching

The Tonight Show when the host, Johnny Carson, read kids' letters to Santa Claus. Louise was intrigued, and she decided to visit the local post office to read a few of the letters that accumulated there, unopened. In reading those letters, she realized that because their families lived in poverty, many of these children wouldn't have any Christmas presents at all.

The thought of those kids' situations disturbed Louise. They were hopeful enough to write a letter to Santa Claus, and yet on Christmas morning they were sure to be disappointed. So she gathered a handful of the letters, and with just a few days before Christmas, she called on her friends and family to help her give some kids a real Christmas. They managed to buy a few toys and get some items donated. Then on Christmas Eve, Louise and her friends distributed gifts to thirteen San Antonio families who would have nothing otherwise.

She didn't realize it at the time, but her vision for showing love to these families would soon become her mission. The friends who had helped her during that first Christmas wanted to do it again, and so the next Christmas, they brought some of their friends. After a few Christmases had passed, Louise became known as "Elf Louise." And during this most recent holiday season, almost a half-century later, she will still be making children smile. Every year her organization, the Elf Louise Christmas Project, distributes gifts to needy families throughout the San Antonio urban area. Last year, more than forty-five hundred volunteers gathered, wrapped, and distributed over nineteen thousand presents to fifty-six hundred homes.[1]

Our vision is nothing more than just a good idea until it becomes our mission. When a family is on a mission together, everyone in that house clearly understands why they really are there. And not only that, everyone around them knows what that mission is also. Louise Locker's friends knew her mission so well that they gave her a nickname. In San Antonio, Elf Louise is readily recognized throughout the city as the lady who has a distinct and effective mission. When the Christmas season comes around every year, people know what Elf Louise will be doing. And they know that she will also provide a place for them to serve others alongside her.

Every Christ-follower has been given a mission, and when your vision guides it, it has clarity and purpose.

> Jesus, undeterred, went right ahead and gave his charge: "God authorized and commanded me to commission you: Go out and train everyone you meet, far and near, in this way of life, marking them by baptism in the threefold name: Father, Son, and Holy Spirit. Then instruct them in the practice of all I have commanded you. I'll be with you as you do this, day after day after day, right up to the end of the age." (Matt. 28:18–20 *The Message*)

Just like he sent his disciples out on their mission, Jesus is sending your family out, too. The vision that he places within your heart requires activity and nurturing. Otherwise, it just wilts, dies, and disappears. If you've ever had to grow a garden in South Texas, you know what that looks like. There's a level of commitment that's required to get that garden to produce during the hot summer months. You watch it, you water it, and you feed it, and all those things require action!

Our kids don't just become adults and then suddenly begin to live out a vision. From the time they're little ones, they learn what that means by watching their family actively participate in their mission. As they grow, parents lead them to a place where they can be a part of it, too. They hear their family talk about their vision and their mission, what it means and why they do it. As parents, this is our mission within a mission. When we show our children what serving looks like, "serving" is no longer an abstract concept. Instead, the word has meaning and flesh-and-blood reality. And from their earliest days, as we create opportunities for them to participate with us, they grow with a mission. Soon our family's vision and mission begin to expand as each child's personality, talents, and passions begin to develop, and they are incorporated into what we do and who we are.

We're very blessed, because we actually love our son-in-law. He is a vital part of our family, our vision, and our mission. Any correspondence that you get from Robbie, written or electronic, is sure to have one phrase attached to the bottom of the page. You'll find it prominently posted on all his social media, and every day you'll hear him say it to his two sons—"Live the vision." Living our vision means making it our mission. When we hear Robbie say it, we recognize that he knows fulfillment comes to those who take the vision beyond a good idea and live it to its fullest. We see him teach their family's vision to his sons. He leads the entire family as they all participate in the work that results from their vision. For the entire family, their vision becomes their mission.

Activating your family's vision, transforming it from nice ideas to world-changing actions, may be the biggest step of faith you will ever take. There are risks involved, and it's never easy to work more responsibilities into your tight schedule. But this has to be a priority, simply because this is what you were created to be. It's the reason God put your family together. It's the greatest lesson you'll ever teach your children, and there is nothing more important that you can invest into their lives.

Robbie's Story

Sometimes God works in very obvious, life-changing ways. This happened to Robbie, right after he finished his first year at East Carolina University, working on an art degree with a job in mind to use his skill in animation.

He had spent his time out of the classroom in a youth ministry internship, and the challenges and the fulfillment of that experience had made Robbie certain that God had another idea for his future. He sought some sound advice from his youth pastor and determined that his calling was to be in youth ministry. He transferred to Oral Roberts University in Tulsa and received his bachelor's degree in pastoral care with an emphasis in youth ministry. He was confident he had made the right decision. God had placed within him a passion for this work, and he confidently moved on to the next step.

Robbie accepted a youth ministry position in Florida and made his way there, taking some bold steps in creating a lively, growing ministry. Students' lives were changed, and he knew that this was what God had intended for him. During this time, he married Annie. He found in her someone who shared his heart for working with teens. Annie began her career as a teacher, shaping young lives in the classroom. And together they worked side by side—serving, teaching, and sharing their lives with students.

After building a strong youth ministry there in Florida, Robbie received a phone call from Annie's home church in Texas. Their youth ministry position was open, and they invited Robbie to come serve on staff. There were some amazing opportunities there, working with a large, vibrant group of teens, a private school into which he would have input, and a church in an area that they were very familiar with. And Annie found a position teaching theater arts in the high school that she had attended. After seeking God's wisdom, they decided this would be a natural next step in Robbie's ministry career.

He continued to develop and extend his ministry to teens, and everything was beginning to seem quite comfortable and fulfilling.

Then something changed, and it became more difficult to see exactly how God was working. Robbie and Annie had their first child, and with his birth came the news that the baby had some medical problems that would last indefinitely. The ministry that Robbie loved couldn't provide the salary or the medical insurance. And he couldn't invest the time that was needed to sustain that ministry because of the requirements of this new baby.

Devastated? At times, Robbie felt that way. How could his calling to youth ministry have been so strong if it was going to be taken away from him? At the very least, he didn't understand why it had happened this way.

He found another job, working for a financial institution. The hours were not as demanding, and his salary and insurance requirements were met there. He was hired to manage a call center, and his job was to motivate and inspire a group of people who were making phone calls all day. Suddenly, it sounded like the same type of investment he had made into the lives of teens, who were often bored by having to spend every day in a classroom. Robbie began to use the same enthusiasm and some of the activities out of his old youth ministry files to inspire this new group. It worked.

These people were appreciative of how Robbie gave of himself to see to it that they were successful. They began to see him as a friend and confidant. And they opened up to him, seeking help and direction for personal difficulties they were encountering in their lives outside the workplace. A new ministry had begun in the marketplace, and Robbie once again experienced fulfillment through another aspect of his vision.

But God wasn't finished yet. Robbie and Annie, and now their two children, started attending a home church. This group has taken on, as a mission, the public high school where Annie is teaching. It's an inner-city school, and most of the students are missing meals because their families either can't provide them or, sadly, they aren't around to take care of their children. So the church provides funds for Annie and Robbie to invite kids to come have dinner with them at a Mexican restaurant in the neighborhood. The restaurant, owned by a Christian family, opens up their private dining room for them. So every Tuesday, over a plate of delicious tacos and enchiladas, Robbie carries on a new extension of his youth ministry. Kids pour into the restaurant, and Robbie and Annie give them the opportunity not only for a meal, but also to share the struggles they are going through as teens in difficult circumstances.

Recently, the home church gave Robbie an opportunity to have a weekend retreat with the students, and seven were baptized, right there in the swimming pool.

We don't always understand the direction that our lives take. Robbie thought that having to leave the typical youth ministry setting was the end of something. But now, in a new, exciting way, he has the opportunity to continue to "live the vision."

Helping the Elf

We herded a load of loud, excited teens onto the bus, and we tried our best to settle them down enough to tell them what the day's agenda would be. There were more than fifty on board, all of them members of the high school's Fellowship of Christian Athletes, and most of that number were rowdy football players. Their larger-than-average bodies were crammed somewhat uncomfortably into the bus seats, and their athletic aggressiveness caused a lot of jostling and friendly shoving and pulling.

Once I finally managed to cool it down to a reasonable level of quietness, I described to them our daylong mission and made clear the level of decorum that would be expected while we were working there. "There will be quite a few other groups working with us," I informed them. "All ages and all kinds of people. Try not to frighten any of the old ladies, please. Have a good time, but be on your best behavior and work hard."

And then I made clear our plan for organization. "If any of you are really good at wrapping packages, there will be a section of the building for you. They need plenty of muscle to move toys around and load them onto trucks, so if you're feeling especially strong today, that's where you'll be. Finally, all of you offensive and defensive linemen—they have Santa costumes for you in the dressing room. Get ready fast and practice your 'ho, ho, hos.'"

The Elf Louise Christmas Project is housed in a large warehouse in an industrial area of San Antonio. It's packed to the ceiling with donated toys in some areas, and at any given time of the day or night, hundreds of volunteers will be scurrying around, focused on getting a very big task done. It's a warm South Texas version of what the workshop at the North Pole would look like. Schools, churches, businesses, civic organizations, and just ordinary families have worked shoulder to shoulder there for decades to make sure that every child in the San Antonio area receives Christmas gifts.

As we had come to expect from this group, our kids rose to the occasion and finished their own assignments there, as well as lending a hand to others who were needing a strong back or youthful enthusiasm. Then we divided up into teams, got into delivery trucks, and headed out for the poverty-stricken areas of our city. Our student population was certainly not affluent, but they were amazed at what they saw when we drove into these neighborhoods.

As we walked the streets there, we were met by groups of small children, thrilled to see the new faces visiting them, especially the bearded man in the red suit. That guy, at six-foot-two and two hundred sixty pounds, had been wreaking havoc on the football field just weeks before, clearing a path for his running back through the defense. Now he knelt there among all the squealing kids, giving out hugs and handing them gifts, with tears running down his cheeks. His life and the lives of all the teenagers we brought there that day had been changed forever.

You can learn more about the Elf Louise Christmas Project, or make a donation at http://elflouise.org.

Focus

What is one thing you could do this week that would be a part of acting on your vision?

Part Four

Making Vision Work

Chapter Sixteen

Your Vision in Your Family

It would be easy to overthink and overspiritualize the idea of discovering a God-inspired vision for our families, to the point that we don't even try. For some reason, we look at others and decide that they are surely more together, more talented, and certainly more holy than we are, and we disqualify ourselves from being useful in God's kingdom before we ever even ask him what he needs us to do.

Somehow, we disconnect the fact that he made each of us unique as snowflakes, loves us for exactly who he created us to be, and has wonderful, powerful ideas for how we spend our lives. And even further, he puts us into these crazy groups we call families, with specific plans for each of us, and a vision for how he wants to use all of us collectively.

But as we discussed in early chapters, without understanding and welcoming his vision, we muddle and bump around and get into each other's way like people intent on making their own peanut butter sandwiches, all reaching for the jelly or the knife drawer at the same time. We often allow chaos to define family life in many, if not all, aspects of our home.

But the first thing to understand is that God wants to guide us, and his desire is to bless us always, in all things. God doesn't play hide-and-go-seek games with his children. Jeremiah 29:13, in *The Message*, holds this promise: "When you come looking for me, you'll find me. Yes, when you get serious about finding me and want it more than anything else, I'll make sure you won't be disappointed."

While we probably shouldn't expect to wake up and find it all spelled out on the dining room wall, or in a burning bush in the backyard, it is possible for every family to confidently take some practical steps toward becoming a family guided by vision.

The process is really organic. We tend to think in terms of those highly visible families, like gospel music's Winans family or the Mannings of football fame, and assume that the task is just too big to achieve anything on that level. But there are as many other possibilities as there are families on earth, and the adventure is in seeing what God will do with the ragtag bunch that shows up in the kitchen at your house every morning, whether it's for a sunny sit-down waffles-and-eggs breakfast together, or a grab-a-bagel-and-run, ships-passing-in-the-night relay.

Start with the answer to this question: Where are you now? For instance, in a military family, mom or dad may be serving, sometimes in places far away from the rest of the family. There may be multiple moves involved for the whole family. Maybe God will develop a vision for serving in support groups for families of people who are deployed, in communities on base, or in communities and cultures overseas. Maybe it will be a commitment simply to pray for those who are deployed and especially in detail for the families they leave at home. Maybe you are comfortable visiting wounded warriors or taking brownies and sitting with their families as they wait. Or maybe it is taking the lead in welcoming and befriending newcomers to your particular base. We've had the opportunity to speak to groups on several military installations, and we've met families at each place that are actively living their vision. It's encouraging to see their dedication to serving, and how much satisfaction it brings to every family that's involved.

Maybe you have more financial resources than you really need and family members who are sensitive to unspoken needs in the lives of those they encounter. Perhaps God wants to use you as secret agents to discover and covertly address the physical needs of people you encounter. The investment you make there will far surpass any savings account or 401(k) that you might deposit the money into. There is a precious family in Tulsa, Oklahoma, whose vision for offering help, hope, and a home to one foster child has unfolded over time to something so large that it is beyond imagination for most of us.

As parents of two children, they were moved to foster a child with special needs that put him beyond the ability of most foster families to care for. But this family, children included, not only met the physical and extensive medical needs of the foster child. They also began to love him as if he were their own, at the same time making it a point to pray for and love the birth parents. As time went by, they felt led to legally adopt the child.

Then came the opportunity to do the same for another foster child with extreme medical needs. Believing that this was what God was asking of them, they brought that child into their home as well, and they found that God was faithful to provide the finances they needed to be able to cover the medical expenses.

At this point, they have four children with extreme medical needs who are at various stages, from foster care to full adoption, of becoming a permanent part of their family. And for each, they have also reached out in love to the birth parents, gently seeking to lead them to Jesus.

Over time, they have paid legal fees for adoption and other processes, and they have seen two of the four through organ transplants. From morning until late at night, there are daily medical routines to attend to for each child, and both of the parents also work to be able to pay for everything the family needs. The physical demands for their care alone would exhaust and overwhelm most families.

And yet they are active in the life of their church, and their posts on Facebook are upbeat, courageous, and filled with hope. A look through their family photo albums shows a large family of six happy, laughing, well-loved kids. Their unique family vision unfolded one child at a time, and it requires an investment of time, love, and hard work from the whole family in order to succeed.

We've seen families who teach, families who run vacation Bible schools, and families who show up on Saturday mornings, unload the mower and trimmer, and all get busy caring for the lawns of people unable to do so themselves. The possibilities are endless. The journey begins taking one step at a time, starting with exactly where you are and who you are today. Who you are as a family, what you do well, and what touches your heart and elicits a natural response, is most likely where your family's vision begins.

As you begin the journey, you can be certain that God will guide you every step of the way. He will use you to change your world at the same time that he enriches your family.

The Winans Family

It was the summer of 1980, and Martha and I had made the two-hundred-mile drive to Houston to see our friend, Andrae Crouch, in concert there. The trip hadn't been easy for Martha, since she was eight months pregnant with our first baby.

As always, Andrae's concert was outstanding. But the best part of the evening would take place afterwards, when we met Andrae in his hotel room. Spending time with him was always inspiring, refreshing, and hilarious, all at the same time. Since Andrae passed away in 2015, we've missed those moments.

Time passed by so quickly in that downtown Houston hotel that it was almost 3:00 A.M. when we decided we should make our way back to San Antonio. "Before you leave, I want you to hear something," Andrae said. He took a cassette player off the desk and pressed the play button. From that now-antique music machine, the voices combined in tight, complex harmonies to produce a distinctive, soulful sound. Even though the recording was raw, there was no doubt that the singers were destined for something great.

"They're four brothers from Detroit, named Winans." he said. "I'm going to get them on my record label." Less than a year later, Marvin, Carvin, Ronald, and Michael Winans released their first recording, *Introducing the Winans*, on the Light label. It was an immediate success, and their international music career was launched. They weren't, however, the first of the Winans family to sing gospel music. Their great-grandfather, Isaiah Winans, was founding pastor of Detroit's Mack Avenue Church of God in Christ in 1919. He was known not only for his dynamic preaching, but also for his booming singing voice.

Isaiah's grandson, David, grew up in that church, and by the time he was a teenager, he was singing in a gospel group known throughout the area, directed by gospel music legend

James Cleveland. It was while he was a part of that choir, the Lucille Lemon Gospel Chorus, that he noticed the pianist, Delores Ransom. They fell in love and were married in the Mack Avenue Church in 1953.

David and Delores, known as Pop and Mom, had ten children, and from the beginning, the entire family made music together. In addition to the four brothers who made up the quartet called The Winans, the other family members were David II, Daniel, Benjamin (BeBe), Priscilla (CeCe), Angelique, and Debra.

In an interview on radio station WLIB in New York City, Marvin talked about what it was like day to day, growing up in the Winans' household. "We sang everything. I mean from television commercials . . . everything. And we always put a gospel spin on it."

"Everybody was always singing, we always had a piano," his twin brother Carvin added. "We'd walk through the house humming and harmonizing. It was all we did."[1]

Marvin said that Mom taught the kids the vocals and instruments, and Pop encouraged them to keep working and kept their focus on the family's vision of sharing God's message through the music.

Pop traveled throughout the area, preaching, while the family sang with him. He put together an annual Christmas concert at Detroit's Mercy Hall, to share his family's music with the community. It wasn't long until Detroit wasn't the only city talking about the Winans. People all over the Midwest were hearing about them, too.

For more than a half a century, various combinations of the siblings have teamed up to sing gospel music. As a duet, BeBe and CeCe have received ten Grammy Awards, twenty-one Dove Awards (from the Gospel Music Association), and fifteen Stellar Gospel Music Awards (from Central City Productions); they have been recognized on Nashville's Music City Walk of Fame and the Hollywood Walk of Fame; and they were inducted into the Gospel Music Hall of Fame. Added to that, the rest of the family has won twelve Grammys, eight Doves, and three Stellars. Mom and Pop were also Grammy nominees for their debut album, *Mom & Pop Winans*, and Mom's solo album, *Hymns from My Heart*, was nominated for two Dove Awards.

Mom and Pop Winans had a vision for their family, and CeCe spoke about it to the *Washington Post*. "We thank God for our parents," she said. "They're why we stayed in the church, and fell in love with the church. They taught us God's word and values and they didn't represent Christian living as being a boring life—they lived it in front of us and showed us they could be happy."[2]

Marvin, one of the original members of the quartet, is the founding pastor of Detroit's Perfecting Church, a thriving congregation that has a vital influence in the community. It was from that church that the Marvin L. Winans Academy of Performing Arts was born. So the family's vision for ministering through gospel music has expanded as the family shares their hearts with others.

The Winans' musical legacy didn't end with the ten siblings. When he was eighteen, Pop and Mom's grandson, Marvin Jr., formed a group called Winans Phase 2 with his cousins, Carvin Jr., Michael Jr., and Juan. Their first release, *We Got Next*, debuted at number one on Billboard's gospel chart, and it was nominated for a Grammy. Juan is also a standout writer, arranger, and producer, and he has been nominated for a Grammy in that category. His cousin Josiah is a producer also.

How can a family, for generations, live out a vision that is so clearly defined? Mom Winans was asked that question in an interview with *B.L.A.C. Detroit* magazine. She answered, "The Bible says, 'Train up a child in the way he should go, and when he is old, he will not depart from it.' That way, they know right from wrong and are hesitant to do wrong. A lot of children are missing that. But it's never too late. God is always there. I don't care what you've done and how you've done it. If you want to do better, he's always there to help you."[3]

Andrae told us in that Houston hotel room that he had a feeling about the Winans, that they were something special. He was exactly right. As we left that evening for the drive back home, he followed us out of the hotel and told Martha, "By the way, that's a baby girl you're carrying." Those were the days before sonograms revealed your unborn baby's gender. But Andrae was right about that, too.

Focus

Has there ever been a time when you think you missed, or ignored, God's leading in your life?

When has there been a time you were certain that God was directing you? What happened as a result?

Chapter Seventeen

Your Vision in Your Church

> "Every day they continued to meet together in the temple courts. They broke bread in their homes and ate together with glad and sincere hearts, praising God and enjoying the favor of all the people. And the Lord added to their number daily those who were being saved."
>
> —*Acts 2:46–47* NIV

A look at the church of the New Testament does not show us people sitting in neat rows on Sunday mornings, listening to concert-quality music, politely hearing a sermon, and then leaving, duty done until the next week. It was a group of people who were completely sold out to Christ and to each other. The church of the New Testament was noted for the love and commitment believers had for one another, and it was engaged in meeting needs of the community and spreading the gospel near and far. It was a gathering of people who were actively involved in living their lives to the very fullest and in giving of themselves literally all that they could give. The church was dynamic and energetic, engaging and magnetic, and sometimes it was even dangerous. You couldn't just hang around on the fringes. You were either all in or you weren't in at all.

While it is possible in today's American church culture to merely attend church, that is not the way to find any of the joy and effectiveness that you read about in the early church. If the only thing you and your family contribute to the church is keeping your pew warm, or even what you place in the offering plate on Sunday morning, then it's time to get excited and get involved. Your involvement within a community of believers will develop your family vision, and it will certainly provide you with creative, engaging ways to weave your vision into the life and vital ministry there.

If your immediate reaction to that statement is a panicked protest that you are not a musician or a public speaker, you can take a deep breath because, remember, your family vision is about exactly who God made and gifted *your* crew to be. The pastor and staff, the choir and praise team, the organist, and the Sunday school teachers, while crucial to the Sunday activities in most churches, are not the only ones necessary to the life of a vibrant congregation. Your church needs you, and every member of your family, in wholehearted commitment to the life that goes on there. And incorporating your family vision there will help you find exactly the gap that you are needed to fill.

For years, we attended church with a wonderful family whose vision had to do with just plain old work, behind the scenes. You would never find these sweet believers in front of a group, leading anything in a public sense, but you did see them everywhere, all over the church campus, on an almost daily basis. Folks in this family committed themselves to seeing that the lawn was mowed and the grounds were kept. Hinges were oiled, walls were painted, broken tables or chairs were repaired, and playground equipment was built. The whole family straightened and prepared the sanctuary and the Sunday School rooms. They were the ones who came early to make the coffee and stayed late to wash out the coffeemaker. Generations of the family—grandparents, parents, and even the kids—were busy in the background, smiling and making sure that the gathering place was ready and waiting for everyone and every use.

Another family made their lovely home and large yard always available for everything from committee meetings to youth group activities, purposefully investing in extra folding chairs and tables, ready for any event. They were there, making everyone who came feel welcome, each of their children learning early to be gracious hosts of people of any age. That sense of hospitality even extended to more than once hosting foreign exchange students in their home over an entire school year. Today that mom, now widowed and in her nineties, still hosts women's groups in her home.

In a family where the mother was a talented designer and seamstress, she made hundreds of costumes for their church's elaborate drive-through live nativity event. Family members pressed costumes, hung and labeled them, transported them, helped assign and fit them to characters, then gathered, laundered, and stored them for the next year, in a labor of love that extended across the entire year.

Is your family drawn to befriending people who seem lonely? Include someone like that in your plans for dinner after the service. And remember, every member of your family should be encouraged to participate in finding someone to minister to, so you might be hosting a great-grandmother one week and a sixth grader the next.

Is your family's heart for foreign missions? Participate in (or take the lead on) fundraisers and drives, or adopt your church's missionaries and commit to pray for them daily as a family. You could also send encouraging emails and the occasional care package.

Do you all like to get in the kitchen together? Volunteer to cook for camp or for your church's ministry to the homeless or for other church gatherings where a meal would be needed.

We know owners of a dry cleaning business who run a clothing ministry for their church. They take used clothes that members donate, dry clean and repair them at their shop, and then organize a "store" area at the church. The family works together there on Saturdays, assisting people in the community as they come to find the clothes they need for themselves and their children.

Are you and your teens good at loving and playing with little ones? What a great thing it would be to run the nursery on Sunday mornings, even for one Sunday a month.

Would it fit your family profile to plant and care for a garden that could supply produce for your church's food pantry? Remember, even if there's someone whose thumb is more gray than green, there is a need in this outreach to wash and sort and deliver the food, too. There's surely a role for everyone.

Is technology your thing? Running sound and video, installing and teaching software, or maintaining computers are all skills that can be a blessing to your pastors, worship leaders, and congregation.

Once you discover the area where your family operates most effectively, think creatively and prayerfully about when, where, and how you can enhance the work and corporate life of the people you worship with. Sit down with your pastor or the appropriate people in church leadership, and let them know of your commitment to being active in the church's ministry. If they aren't already aware of your gifts and interests, let them get to know about you, and then discuss how your abilities fit into the church's plan for ministry.

Your family will grow together as you apply your unique assets and see how you bless others and glorify God in doing so. You might be surprised to see how your attitudes about church change, and your family roles there will be more fulfilling and effective than ever before.

Focus

Are you committed to a specific church at this time? If not, why not?

If you are not part of a church now, make a list of the characteristics that would be important to you and your family, and start looking! If you are an active part of a church, what needs do you see there that you and your family could fill, even part-time?

Be creative in thinking of ways your family might contribute to the life, fellowship, or ministry of your church. Include your kids in the brainstorm session, too. You could also ask a pastor or other church leader for ideas about where to get involved.

Chapter Eighteen

Your Vision in Your Career

You've got your missionaries, you've got your pastors, and you've got your music and youth directors. Those are the people who are in the ministry. A lot of times, it seems that all other occupations are considered secular. And while it is a good thing to support your family, and to have a career, your job does not necessarily have anything to do with your spiritual life. Or just maybe, it has everything to do with it.

The truth is, when we are guided by the vision God gives us for living our lives in his way, every aspect of our days will be part of that vision, including our work. And eventually, as we live out our vision within our families, it will affect not only how we operate in the workplace but also our attitudes toward work and, possibly, even the eventual career choices of our children.

Certainly any vision God has for our families would include complete integrity, honest investment of effort, and the exhibition of unfailing respect and kindness to those we work for and with.

But it will also involve more than that. Vision recognizes that we are not at our workplace by accident, and it requires us to operate in that arena according to God's design and call on our lives. As we begin to understand how God has gifted us and how he wants to use us from day to day, we will be drawn to the people, places, and tasks where we can best contribute for him.

There is much joy to be found in knowing that, with God, any and every job becomes a holy calling. The opportunity for "full time ministry" is wherever we are, and our attitudes and actions in that realm will undoubtedly influence our children as they make decisions and choices for their adult lives. Have you noticed how often children grow up and follow in the footsteps of their mother's or father's career? This happens not necessarily because of plans or pressure from us as parents, but simply because it becomes a life habit to use vision as the compass that directs our choices in life.

When we make career choices that mesh with our vision, a sense of satisfaction and fulfillment about the work we're doing will almost always follow. Your children, as well as the rest of the people in your world, will sense that and be drawn to what you do. It won't be because the work is so attractive, but they will respond to what they see in you as you do what you're doing. It's not an attitude that you can make happen. Instead, it's a heartfelt contentment that you will possess. Work is never intended to be easy. That's why we call it *work*. But an overwhelming sense of peace will be evident as your career meshes with your calling.

An Open Door

Greg's parents were guided by a vision for caring for people, whoever they were and wherever they encountered them.

As a sales representative for a dairy, Greg's dad befriended a widower who was raising a large family of children alone, supporting them by operating a small family grocery store. Dad had made it a habit to take ice cream treats, or perhaps the occasional bounty of a successful fishing trip, whenever he called there. Years later, we encountered one of those children who, as an adult, not only remembered those visits but had made a career of teaching and caring for low income students. He made it a point to tell us what those visits had meant to him as a child.

Dad had a knack for knowing just what people needed at the time. He was well-known for showing up with a pot of homemade potato or vegetable soup if he knew someone was under the weather. He heard that one man had been diagnosed with extremely low potassium levels, and before an hour had passed, he was delivering a big bag of bananas. Hearing a little girl at church, one of six siblings, expressing her desire for a desk of her own at home, he began to search bargain stores, and sure enough, before the end of the week, he was delivering a white desk that was the perfect size for her to use.

People who were hospitalized would be cheered to see Dad's grin as he stuck his head in the door of their room after he had finished work and pulled up a chair for a visit. Families who filled surgery waiting rooms could always rely on the quiet comfort of his presence as he sat with them through those tension-filled hours. Upon retirement from the dairy, Greg's dad took on official responsibility for the pastoral care of church members, visiting those who were hospitalized or new to the community, simply carrying on the vision he had been living out every day already.

Meanwhile, Greg's mother worked many years as a headhunter for a national firm, where she recruited qualified applicants for companies with job openings to fill.

When she found someone who might qualify for a specific job opening, she worked with that person to develop a resume and to prepare for the job interview, covering everything from what to wear and how to shake hands to practicing answers to possible questions. Her warm acceptance and encouraging manner caused people to open up to her and talk freely about their lives.

On a regular basis, helping applicants prepare for a job interview turned into helping them with other life needs, and they often ended up at the family dinner table that evening. It was not unusual for dinner with the family to lead to meaningful conversations, prayer, and an invitation to attend church the next Sunday. Numerous people made their first step into the kingdom of God over a bowl of Ma's dumplings or chicken spaghetti, and many a single person or newlywed couple, far from their own families on holidays, found the sense of home and family that they longed for in the caring warmth and welcome that Greg's parents created in their home.

As each parent lived out the family vision at work, their children observed, and those actions and attitudes communicated that vision to them as well. Because their vision became a part of their children's life, the habit of opening home and hearts to others has carried into our home, too.

Both of Greg's parents are now with the Lord, but their approach to loving people lives on. The front door of Greg's childhood home, through which so many people came and went to receive the ministry and blessing that his parents offered on a daily basis, now hangs at the entrance to our home, a symbolic celebration of who his parents were, and a sweet reminder of our privilege of continuing that heritage.

A great example of how vision can influence generations in their choices of vocation and careers can be found in the roots of the Singleton clan, beginning with Greg's grandparents. They raised ten children on a farm in North Texas during the Depression, and making ends meet enough to provide even the basics in food and clothing was a daily challenge to their faith and persistence. However, the children all grew up seeing their mom and dad not only provide for their large family, but also care for the needs of others in the community, even if it meant some sacrifice for themselves. Their generosity didn't go unnoticed by those who had received it. At one point, the entire Singleton family was stricken with smallpox, and they were all under quarantine. The members of their community took turns bringing meals to them, leaving the food down at the creek near their house, for whatever sibling was feeling strongest to go and fetch.

At a recent reunion of all thirty cousins and their children and grandchildren, we were struck by the fact that a majority of those descendants today are in careers that involve serving other people. Pastors, missionaries, educators, first responders, and directors or advocates for nonprofit organizations fill the ranks of the family today, continuing to live out the family vision of caring for others established by that original family.

So, as God's vision for our families begins to unfold, we should understand that our work will not be separate from it. Instead, the place where we spend such a large part of our days will surely be affected in positive ways as we operate within his plan and calling. The same thing holds true for parents on the job and the children in school. And every member of our family will be enriched by the experience.

As you explore what God's vision looks like for your family, consider how it will influence the work you do each day.

"All God's Children Got Shoes!"

Toms Shoes burst onto the scene in 2006, creating an instant sensation not only in fashion, but also in business.

Along with the trendy, comfortable design of the shoes, the idea of giving one pair of shoes to a child in a developing country for every pair the company sold appealed to American consumers, and it was immediately so successful that other companies took note and soon began to adopt the innovative, creative, and philanthropic business model for their products.

Blake Mycoskie is the young entrepreneur whose vision has profoundly affected the marketplace, in addition to providing shoes, and now eyeglasses, to well over fifty million children living in poverty both in America and worldwide.

The story of how he was inspired to start his company has been widely featured in the media and on company videos. While on vacation in Argentina, Blake had seen that most of the children were barefoot, and many suffered from the health problems that going without shoes can cause. As an entrepreneur, he had noticed the shoe the native workers wore and had wondered how a version of that shoe might sell in the United States. As the son of a doctor, he had concerns about the widespread health problems he observed in the children of the village in which he was staying.

Sitting on a hill, watching the children playing, and thinking about the scene, Blake came up with the idea for his business. When he returned from that trip, he boldly set about making the vision a reality, and within a year, he and his employees were back in South America, making their first "shoe drop."

But Blake's story as a visionary businessman and philanthropist has its roots in his parents' home in Texas, where he grew up. Even as a youngster, he was always coming up with creative ideas for businesses. He had a knack for recognizing a need for goods or services and coming up with ways to make money by meeting it. As a college student, he created a service that would do laundry for students living in dorms on campus. That business became so successful that he was soon able to sell it for profit, the first of several business ventures, some of which were more successful than others.

"My parents always supported me and encouraged me to go ahead and take risks," Blake told us in an interview. "If something didn't work out, they never called it failure. They helped me look for the positive takeaway and figure out what I could learn from the experience."

Growing up, Blake saw what his parents valued as he watched them from day to day.

"Dad was a doctor," Blake said, "and he was all about taking care of people. I began to realize that he was caring for people who had no way of paying him, along with those who could pay. He was a very humble person.

"And my mom had the most giving heart," he said. "She was volunteering all the time."

So meeting needs of people whenever and wherever he saw them and stepping out with boldness and creativity in business became the perfect combination for Blake that afternoon in Argentina. "I had always thought I would spend the first part of my life making money," he said, "and the last part giving it away. But I realized you don't have to put giving on hold. It's something Christ did. You build giving into your life from the very beginning. Even as a carpenter, he gave of himself in service every day. Anyone can do that."

From the home of parents with a vision to do what they could to meet the needs of their community, to a son with a vision to meet the basic needs of impoverished children across the world, came a radically innovative business model that has inspired numerous corporations to look for ways to make social responsibility part of their business plan.

That's how God works through a family's vision.

Focus

Think about the work situations of every family member who has a job. What opportunities already exist for you to be a positive presence, a kind presence, an encourager to people as you work?

What can you do to creatively expand your positive influence there?

Chapter Nineteen

Your Vision in Your Finances

"*Beauty and the Beast* is coming to the Majestic in January, and I want us to go and take the kids so they can experience live theater."

"How much will that cost?"

"Tickets are eighty-five dollars each. But we can put them on my credit card."

"If we take the kids, that's too much to add to the card."

"Baylor is bowl-eligible this year! The minute tickets go on sale, we'll get some!"

"But won't we have to fly there and get a hotel and all that, too?"

"Oh, come on! This doesn't happen that often. We can tailgate with our friends. It will be fun. We need to have fun."

"I was thinking it would be so perfect if we could give Abby a new car for graduation. What do you think?"

"I think we can't afford a new car and tuition, too."

"Well, it might be a squeeze for us, but just think how cute she would be driving around Austin in a burnt-orange Wrangler!"

"I think a used car that she helps pay for would be a better idea."

"We've had this house for ten years. I want to remodel the kitchen. New cabinets, granite countertops, tile backsplash, and new appliances."

"That's going to cost a bundle, and what we have is just fine. Besides, I thought we were going to buy a boat so we could spend weekends at the lake, fishing."

"Our tax return money came today. It's enough to put new tires on the truck and have all of the oak trees trimmed."

"Wait! I was counting on us going shopping to get a new couch and chair for the living room!"

Talking about how much money we have, and what we are going to do with it, can get tricky, even just within the confines of a marriage. Almost every marriage expert agrees that finances cause more arguments between a husband and wife than any other issue. But as your family's vision begins to direct how you live, your finances invariably become involved.

It is really easy in today's culture to fall into the all-too-common want-it, get-it habit. But this attitude leads us to build up debt that can limit our ability to freely and fully serve God.

As you begin to live out your family's vision, and your daily life takes on new meaning and direction, your budget will come into play as well.

Romans 12:1–2, in *The Message*, puts it this way:

> So here's what I want you to do, God helping you: Take your everyday, ordinary life—your sleeping, eating, going-to-work, and walking-around life—and place it before God as an offering. Embracing what God does for you is the best thing you can do for him. Don't become so well-adjusted to your culture that you fit into it without even thinking. Instead, fix your attention on God. You'll be changed from the inside out. Readily recognize what he wants from you, and quickly respond to it. Unlike the culture around you, always dragging you down to its level of immaturity, God brings the best out of you, develops well-formed maturity in you.

The message of this Scripture may cause you to reconsider your spending and rearrange some of your budget in order to develop gifts and talents you see in family members, or to enable you to go places and do things that allow you to live out your vision. It may mean that those funds that were intended simply for pleasure might have to be used for something different.

We know a family who cares deeply about foreign missions and who focused much prayer and interest on the situations and needs of various areas in the world. They were constantly conducting fundraisers, teaching their kids to mow lawns, bake cupcakes, wash cars, or clean houses in order to raise money. They also saved and invested family funds to ensure that each of their six children had more than one experience on short-term mission trips to various places in the world. The parents, both of whom had careers in medical fields, also made a point of taking different children with them as they participated in medical missions. A large part of the family budget each year supported those trips, but the kids also learned the joy of working to earn and then invest in their family vision.

If your vision involves hospitality, then you will probably want to adjust your grocery budget to allow for extra coffee and desserts, or for guests to eat dinner with you.

Or perhaps you will want to have some funds free each month to hit the dollar store for socks and small toiletries to include in the sacks of canned food, snacks, and water that you keep in your car to give to homeless people you encounter, if that is part of your vision.

Maybe you will need to allow for the cost of team sports for your kids, as a way of making your whole family available in friendship to other families in your community.

Or on a larger scale, perhaps your vision will have you planning for investment in certain nonprofit organizations or real estate or business projects that will be a means of accomplishing God-given goals.

And sometimes, it will take long-term financial planning to be able to bring parts of your vision to life. A couple we know who began their marriage as Bible translators in Africa returned to the United States to raise their family. Over the years, they were able to go, with their kids, on various short-term missions. But as they worked, he as a pastor and she as a teacher, they were planning, saving, and investing with their vision in mind. They recently retired, were able to build a cabin in Colorado, and now spend half of each year in Africa, again working with Bible translators. The other half of the year, they host their children and grandchildren in their cabin.

We are instructed to bring our tithes into the storehouse of the church, for the life and outreach of the congregation we are part of. That is a priority and is certainly a necessary financial discipline. And that, the Scripture tells us, is to be done joyfully. But, in addition to that, as our family vision begins to define our life's activities and our passion for following and serving Christ, our priorities will dictate how we apply our budgets.

Invested for Inheritance

As they drove the dark highway toward their home near Seattle late one night, Jon and Jo were in a pensive, reflective mood.

They had just spent the weekend closing up Jo's parents' estate following their untimely deaths. Thinking of her upbringing by Christian parents, and of Jon, who also had a strong heritage of faith passed down for generations from an ancestor who had been a pastor in Sweden, she asked Jon, "Both my mom and dad, and yours, were successful in transferring their spiritual values and beliefs to us, but they never sat us down and said, 'This is what we believe.' Yet we adopted their faith as our own. How did they do that?"

Miles passed, and then Jo mused aloud, "Are we doing as good a job as they did?

Our kids are in high school now. What more do we need to do? We are not called to be certain that they have success or money. We are simply called to pass down our values to our children."

After his successful career as a pharmacist in the Air Force, they had returned to Washington, where Jo taught school and Jon rejoined his family in the pharmacy business. They had enjoyed and benefitted from working together as a family through the years, and they wanted to be sure that the sense of belonging and unity were preserved for their children as well.

Years passed, and as their children became adults with careers and families of their own, Jo continued to teach, and Jon followed what he sensed was God's direction to spend a number of years in church administration and oversight for their denomination, which had included some experience in building houses as a part of the church's missionary outreaches.

In 2004, Jon retired from the nearly twenty-five years he had spent in church work, and he began helping their son, Chad, as they financed and built houses. In February of 2008, the father and son were guests at a Super Bowl party that was going to impact their family in ways they could never have imagined. At halftime, their host, Craig, showed a video about a group of high school students who spent their spring break building a house for a family in Mexico.

"I was so amazed by what had happened for those teens that I didn't even pay attention to the second half," Jon said. "Instead, I stood in a hallway having a conversation with Chad about how cool that was. We decided that we needed to do something like that with our construction crew."

They spent the rest of that year talking and thinking about how they could begin building houses for families in need in Mexico. Then one night, Jon had a vivid dream.

"In the dream, Chad and I and some others were building houses in Mexico. I could see the joy on the faces of little children who were gathered around watching us," he said. "The next morning, I boldly told our crew, 'Guys, we are going to start an adventure this year!'"

"The construction company had built and sold about one hundred houses and had invested in property for future development," Jon said. "But at about that time, the housing market tanked, leaving us with twelve unsold houses and heavy financial worries and concerns. But the desire to build houses in Mexico persisted."

One particular day, as they were wrestling with how they would handle the unsold inventory and the construction loans they needed to repay, Chad looked his dad in the eye and said, "It's going to be okay. We need to go to Mexico."

"How can we, with the unsold houses?" Jon asked.

"Relax, Dad," Chad said.

So they went to Mexico for a weekend to observe a church doing homebuilding there. They learned about a group called Baja Christian Ministry, which would identify families in need, buy the property, lay the concrete foundation, and deliver the precut lumber to the site.

"We realized that we could come in, build a house, and be out in eight hours," Jon said.

Not long after, Chad's older brother Jeremy called him. "You need to hear about what the company Toms Shoes is doing," he told his brother.

Chad immediately called his dad. "You need to look at this video on YouTube, about the business model for Toms Shoes," he said, "and call me right back."

That was the first Jon had heard of the company, which provides a pair of shoes free to a child in a developing country for every pair of shoes sold in the United States.

When Jon called back, Chad said, "Dad, I think we need to build a house in Mexico for every house we build here. Not sell. Build!"

"We don't have enough profit built in for that, Chad," Jon replied.

"We've got twelve houses sitting unsold, Dad. What do we have to lose?" Chad asked.

Jon's answer was simple, and he surprised himself. "I'm on board."

What happened next was beyond their imagination.

"Once we committed to one another," Jon said, "ten of those houses sold in one month! The other two we rented to college students, which gave us a nice steady flow of income."

In the beginning, as they built a house in the States, the family would take the construction crew down to Mexico and build a house there. They developed a pattern of building the house on a Friday, turning over the keys to the family that evening. On Saturday, they would go door to door, inviting people in the *colonia* to a hot dog feed, to hear some good news, and to receive a gift.

"We were so surprised, in the beginning, when almost the whole village would show up," Jo exclaimed. "With an interpreter, one or two of us simply tell what Jesus's love means to us, and tell them that Jesus loves them, too. We ask who wants to know more about Jesus, and people raise their hands. Then we give them each a Bible and a Bible study guide."

"Often, there are people in a village who are already believers, and they step forward and offer to lead Bible study in their homes," Jon added. "Now we have also built churches for the villages where there is a need."

After they had built a few houses in this manner, Chad was doing the final walk-through with a customer on a house they had built in the States.

"Congratulations!" he told her. "When you bought this house, you also just built a house for a family in Mexico."

"She was so excited by the idea that she went ahead and bought another house for her son, too," Jon said.

Over the years, customers began to ask to be included in the actual building, and so Jon and Chad worked out a way for them to go along and be part of the builds. Both sons, their daughter, their spouses, and their children also participate on a regular basis. At a meeting before the Saturday hot dog feed, the team was deciding who would give testimonies that day, when their eight-year-old granddaughter, Gwen, timidly volunteered. But later in the day, she told her grandmother that she was scared.

"I don't know what to say!"

"It's simple, sweetie," Jo told her. "Just tell them that you love Jesus."

Sure enough, that evening when Gwen's turn came, she told the people gathered, "My name is Gwen. I love Jesus, and you need to love him, too."

When their grandson, who is twelve, got back from church camp one summer, the first thing he told the family was, "I can hardly wait to go to Mexico, to give my testimony!"

"My goal now," Jon said, "is to make sure that every dime we spend is somehow connected with our mission."

Focus

Look at your financial statements over the past six months, and consider these questions:

Other than our tithe, what are we investing in our family vision?

If we need, want, or are led to do more, where are some places we could adjust our spending in order to accomplish that?

Chapter Twenty

Your Vision in Your School

Perhaps one of the most difficult decisions parents make is where they will send their children to school. There are many factors to be weighed, from the desire to teach them a Christian worldview or the sense of needing to protect them from threats in the secular culture, to what the family budget and time constraints will allow. As your family vision unfolds, it will influence choices in deciding where and how to educate each child.

The first thing to know is that, despite the strong voices in our American Christian culture that would advocate for one choice or the other as the only correct way, there really is no one venue that is always right for every child in every family, or always wrong for every child in every family. The important thing to understand is that, wherever your children are being educated, parents bear the majority of the responsibility for investing daily in supporting, guiding, and enriching learning for the family.

The thing you can be certain of is that, if you are trying to live out God's vision, he can be trusted to guide and bless and protect and prosper your children. He wants you to lead and guide your kids through their education. And since God's vision is tailor-made for exactly who your family is, individually and as a whole, there will be a wonderful way for you to operate within your school community.

We know a family whose vision includes operating a restaurant in a tourist area as a means of missions outreach. For them, combining homeschooling with giving every child responsibility for working in some area of the business works perfectly. Another family we know educates their children at home in order to allow them all to be part of regular foreign mission trips that the dad leads several times a year.

If performing arts or sports plays a role in your vision, then homeschooling could allow you to tailor times for academics to allow for private music or dance lessons, or for participation in city sports leagues. Homeschooling can also allow time for extra emphasis and research in one particular area of study that will train family members for future endeavors.

If your children are attending a private Christian school, you will probably be able to find other families whose vision is similar to yours, providing a great opportunity to join forces on some projects or outreach ventures. The exchange of ideas and the encouragement would be beneficial for all, and the common beliefs and values of most families at the school could be a source of support for your family as well.

A family with a vision for bringing the Good News to those who have not heard it, or for working to meet the needs of those who may be overlooked in the community, might find that the public school is a mission field where they are needed. It may be more of a stealth operation, but participating in PTA and attending sporting events and concerts opens the door, for both parents and kids, to knowing people you might never find at church. Or if your vision is to be a family of prayer warriors, then just knowing situations of others gives you many concerns to bring before the Father in prayer.

Educating our children well is an important responsibility, because it is part of preparing them to be effective in whatever God will call them to do and to be as adults, so there is an obvious focus on the future. But we are also called to live in the present moment, open always to obeying the lead of the Holy Spirit's gentle prompting.

Living out our family's vision will involve both the means and content of our children's education, and how we use the opportunities that whatever process we choose will bring. And while we can certainly count on God's guidance and blessing as we seek to do that, there are also some inherent pitfalls in each of the situations that we must guard against.

If we teach our children at home, we must be certain that we are not merely insulating them from what we consider evil. Jesus befriended sinners, without himself ever joining in their sin. Instead, he offered compassion, love, and ultimately redemption to all people. Our children need to understand the world, and develop hearts that break with what breaks the heart of God. If we don't take care to include deep issues in our curriculum, but simply aim to protect them from any encounter outside our safety zone, we are actually setting them up to be ineffective in the time to come.

If Christian school is the right place for our kids, we must guard against a kind of complacency that tells us all is automatically well. Just because they are in a Christian school, there is no guarantee that every classmate will be making healthy choices or will automatically want to honor God in all relationships and activities. There must be conversations at home about how to handle relationships and social situations in ways that are not judgmental but that come out of a place of spiritual strength and righteousness. Those are things that only parents can instill.

And if we send our children to public school, whether it is in the most desirable suburb, or in the poverty-stricken inner city, we must take care that they know beyond doubt that they are loved and supported by both God and their family, and that they see themselves on a holy mission, to live out the vision there. It is crucial to send them out every morning having prayed over them and talked through how God might be planning to use them that day.

Whatever the vision that your family is living out, it will offer a guideline as you choose the best place for your children to learn. Wherever that is, as a parent you will play a crucial role in discovering effective ways to enhance your kids' learning and their school experience. God's vision for your family will certainly be a guide for you in the process, and his presence and protection will be a blessing to you and to all you encounter as you go.

Whatever You Need

For Sylvia and Pete, it had its roots in their own childhoods.

Pete's mom was widowed young, with four small boys to raise. She worked hard at a tortilla factory, and she took in sewing and laundry to provide for her sons.

"But I remember that whatever I needed for school, she managed to get for me," Pete recalled. "She even bought me a two-hundred-dollar trombone for the school band."

It was the same for Sylvia. Both of her parents did what was necessary to be able to supply everything she needed in order to complete her education.

"If I needed it for school," she said, "there was no question. They would see to it that I had it."

They each acknowledge the role that adult mentors played for them in their teen years, offering advice and guidance in planning and preparing for their futures where their parents' experience stopped.

"I was very involved in the YWCA (Young Women's Christian Association), and began to volunteer there when I was in high school," Sylvia recalled. "One of the women who worked there took me under her wing, and she put me to work helping her with projects.

"There were so many children who were living in poverty, and she was concerned that they never had gifts at Christmas. She had the post office give her all of the letters to Santa, and she went to work trying to get the gifts for all of them. She would have me busy organizing lists, wrapping presents, and making deliveries. Her project grew into the Elf Louise organization, and I learned so much about volunteering and giving from her."

As Sylvia neared her last year in high school, her mentor took a special interest in her plans and helped her apply for colleges and scholarships, playing a major role in helping Sylvia attend Trinity University.

Meanwhile, Pete was able to attend junior college and then joined the Navy. After leaving the Navy, he earned his bachelor's degree and began teaching high school. As a teacher, he understood when his students did not have the funds for the necessary supplies, and he always found a way to get them what they needed.

The two married, and after a few years, Pete went into business, and he and Sylvia shared an office. Enjoying professional success, when their daughter Esmeralda came along, they decided to set up offices at their home in order to be available for her as their first priority.

From kindergarten on, the first thing they would do each school year was ask for a meeting with each of Esme's teachers. In the course of laying the foundation for a positive relationship, they always made it a point to ask the teachers what was needed for the classroom.

"We would tell them, 'Whatever you need, just tell us, and we will work to get it for you,'" Pete said. "And we would say, 'If there are kids in the class who don't have what they need, please just let us know, and we'll see to it that they have it.'"

The years passed, and as Esme made her way through elementary school and middle school, Pete and Sylvia were always active and involved. Pete was an officer in the PTA and became a leader in their neighborhood association, while Sylvia volunteered and participated in museum associations and book clubs, and they encouraged Esme to be active in a variety of organizations, too. Their home was often the gathering place for those meetings and a location for Esme and her friends to do homework or work together on school projects. Esme joined Youth for Christ, and soon their home was the official meeting place each week.

By the time Esme began attending the public high school, she was already at the head of her class in academics, and she was a student others naturally looked to for leadership roles. Under her influence and with the support of her parents, who opened an effective line of communication with the principal, weekly Youth for Christ meetings were relocated to the campus, and the group became a strong presence.

As often happens, Pete and Sylvia's home in a lovely, established neighborhood became surrounded by other areas and apartment complexes that did not fare so well, so many of Esme's classmates were dealing with the extra problems and issues that come with poverty. When Pete told Esme's teachers that he and Sylvia wanted to help meet other students' needs, the project began to involve much more than pencils, paper, and field trip fees.

"The kids would come to our house because we were there," Sylvia said. "We always had snacks and soda and water out, and whatever else they needed."

"We would tell them, 'If you need to make copies or send a fax or use the computer, just come into our office,'" Pete said. "Whatever you need, you can use it."

"And then we would always have supper," Sylvia said. "We would have a full meal, and sit down at the table, and we would pray. Whoever was there was invited to eat."

It was important to them to provide Esme with as many rich and varied experiences as possible, so they were regulars at museums, concerts, and the theater, and they travelled extensively. As time went by, they began to include Esme's friends in the excursions as well, particularly the ones who would not have those experiences otherwise. Recognizing that some of the boys were lacking a father's guidance and influence, Pete began to take them fishing at the coast, or camping.

"When the kids were at our house, we didn't only feed them," Sylvia said. "I asked them about their homework and questioned them about their plans for after high school. If there was something like an honor society induction, I asked them if they had what they needed to wear. If the boys needed a dress shirt or shoes, we made sure they had them, and we made sure they knew that we would be there, cheering and clapping for them, just like we did for Esme.

"But we had rules, too," Sylvia said. "The boys had to take off their shoes, and I would get after them about sitting back with the chairs on two legs. We taught them table manners, and they knew if they spent the night on Saturday, I would be waking them up early and they would be going to church with us on Sunday."

When it was time for the teens to consider what they would do after high school, Pete and Sylvia began initiating one-on-one conversations and career and education counseling with them.

"We tried to help them figure out what they were good at, what they enjoyed, and what realistic options they had," Pete said. "For some, it was guiding them toward finding a good job that could turn into a career, or the military. For others, we needed to help them see that college was a possibility and walk them through the steps of choosing the right one, applying for admission, and applying for scholarships and financial aid. We spent a lot of time sitting at the computer with them, talking them through it all. And if they didn't have the money to pay the application fee, we were happy to do that for them."

In the spring of their senior year, the stepfather of one of the boys kicked him out of the house. Pete talked to the step-dad and arranged for the boy to live with them for the rest of the year. Sylvia would drive the young man to his night job and pick him up when he was through. When the young man walked the stage at graduation, no one in his family was there to see it. But Pete and Sylvia were.

With Esme graduated and off to college, her parents could have relaxed and pursued their own interests. But instead, they made themselves available to the next class, spending several days a month in the school career center, presenting seminars or giving the same one-on-one guidance that had been so helpful to others before them.

Largely due to the encouragement and assistance the students had found in Pete and Sylvia's home, and Esme's caring to bring her friends to her parents when she knew they had needs, dozens of young adults are finishing college, serving successfully in the military, or working in career pathway jobs, headed for meaningful, useful lives they might have missed without the hope, encouragement, guidance, and support Pete and Sylvia supplied.

For Sylvia and Pete, the words "whatever you need" have been like pebbles dropping into a pond, creating ever-widening circles of blessing that will continue to influence the world.

Focus

What are our goals for our kids' education?

Where are those best met?

How can both parents and kids apply our vision to the area of education?

Chapter Twenty-One

Your Vision in Your Neighborhood

One day, a group of lawyers and great thinkers engaged Jesus in a theological conversation, thinking they were brilliant enough to trap him in some kind of misguided error. Their question had to do with his opinion about God's law, and what specifically was the most important part of it. They assumed Jesus would do a thoughtful, reflective search of the Ten Commandments, and whatever one he selected, they would challenge. But he surprised them. His first answer was to love God with all of your heart, and that one they could hardly argue with. But then he said there was another that was equally important, which was to love your neighbors. Whatever your family vision entails, there is one part of it that you must be sure to attend to. Jesus was specific when he said, in that discussion, "Love your neighbor."

When it comes to exercising our family vision, what better way to start than by loving the folks in our own zip code? And once we begin to dive into the details, we discover that showing love to those right around us calls for a bigger commitment than we might have imagined at first.

If loving our neighbor means more than harboring feelings of general good will and occasionally throwing the newspaper onto the porch for them, then it presents a challenge, given how today's culture tends to isolate families. Generations ago, moms would chat at the clothesline, dads would stop the mower for a visit, and kids in the neighborhood were in and out of each other's houses all day, every day. Mom bought Kool-Aid and cookies to share with the neighbor kids, and she had special rules like, "When they start to eat dinner, don't hang around on the porch. You need to come home." It was easy to know and love the people living nearby.

But today, the more likely scenario is that no one is really around in the daytime. Both parents are at work, the kids are in school or at child care, and in the evenings everyone is either hunkered down in the house, recharging for more of the same tomorrow, or out at sports practice and ballet lessons or Bunko night. A friendly wave as we herd the crew into cars in the morning might be the limit of relationship with our neighbors.

So the question for our families is probably not so much whether we will love our neighbors but, "How we can love our neighbors?"

We've all seen the ad where the weird neighbor couple shows up at the front door with a casserole and awkward questions, and we don't want to be those people. So, how can we make our family a blessing to our neighbors?

The logical place to start is prayer. We can pray for the families that occupy the houses on our street, or the apartments in our building. We don't have to know anything about them, really, to begin praying for protection and blessing and peace in their homes.

We like to go for a brisk walk every morning, and as we stride past houses in our subdivision, we often pray for the people who live there. Without knowing, or even having ever seen, those families, we begin to sense caring for them, our prayers opening our hearts to what our Father feels for each one.

Walking at the same time every morning, we began to recognize people as they headed out to work, exchanging the obligatory Texas nod and hand lift as they passed. If you're not sure what we're talking about, then you haven't spent any time on country roads in our state. The more we walked and prayed, the easier it became to pray for them. One of the teenagers is always at the school bus stop with her book bag and violin case. On the day that she was also juggling her long black dress in a clear garment bag, we just said, "Concert tonight? Cool. Good luck!" as we passed by. Her smile that day, and every day afterward, told us she enjoyed the encouragement.

The next step is to consider our neighborhood on a deeper level. What are the needs here? The homes where we live are getting older, and so are many of the people who occupy them. We see that some of our neighbors might just appreciate having their trash cans rolled back up to the house on collection days, or need the security of having our phone number if they need help fast.

Because our vision includes hospitality, we try to invite our neighbors into our home for occasional dessert and coffee get-togethers, offering a way to get to know and understand each other, and to make ourselves available. It would be almost creepily awkward to offer our phone number to the widow around the corner, with whom we've never shared conversation, but it is natural, in a neighborhood social setting, to say, "Here's our number. If you need something, please call us."

Look at the places where you can participate in the life of your neighborhood. You are wanted and needed at your local school's PTA, whether your kids are in school there or not. Do you run into neighbors at the grocery store, at Starbucks, at local restaurants? What would it look like to put your vision to work in those places?

We are not suggesting that you carry a stack of gospel tracts with you, sticking them into the hands of all you encounter, or hiding them in all of the mailboxes on your street. But we are suggesting that you look up, and look around, and offer friendship and encouragement and service to the people you encounter in your 'hood, and simply be willing to love them, as Christ told us to.

But They Are So Pretty!

As a little girl, I grasped the principle of loving my neighbors. One morning when I was about five, and all of my playmates were already in school, I collected a bag full of cool rocks from a vacant lot next door. I asked my mom if I could paint them, and all too happy to keep me occupied as she tended to the new baby in the family, she set me up on the porch with paints and brushes.

I began, with overflowing creativity and big plans, to decorate a rock for each mom on our block. There was one mom in particular whom I really loved, because she always lavished me with positive attention. So I lavished her rock with *lots* of paint.

The minute I finished painting, I put the rocks in my wagon and set out to deliver my gifts. The homes in our block had been built with mail slots, where the mailman (term of the day) could poke the letters through, and they landed on the living room floor, so that "rain, sleet, or hail" need not be a factor in either delivering or picking up the mail.

I went on my merry way, poking rocks dripping with wet paint through the slots and onto the carpets of our unsuspecting neighbors. It wasn't long until my mom started getting phone calls, the first from the neighbor whose rock I had taken pains to make most special.

I can still remember my mom asking me, "Why did you *do* that? Mrs. Lemons is always so *nice* to you!"

From that experience, I learned that it's good to consider what my neighbors might really need and want before I start just dropping things into their living rooms.

We know a group of young families who, upon graduating from university together, discovered a common vision for their families to make a difference in one of the most impoverished, hopeless, and overlooked areas of Austin. They purposefully bought homes in that area and carefully, prayerfully, enrolled their children in the neighborhood public school, which was desperately low-performing. And then they began to love their neighbors.

They joined the PTA and volunteered to tutor at the school. They included the neighbors' kids as they worked with their own at home to make up for the gaps they were experiencing in instruction at school. They got to know children and their parents and offered love, and hope, and began to model solid marriages and concerned parenting. Within only a couple of years, that school's performance rating skyrocketed.

They befriended their neighbors, invited them to their homes, and shared God's love with them. Some began to meet in homes for Bible study. Others helped adults search for jobs and prepare for interviews. They helped out by watching children while their parents went to work or took classes that would lead to better jobs. In short, they moved there with purpose and simply began to love their neighbors. The result of those decisions has been that the lives of all families in that neighborhood have been enriched, and many families have come to know and love Jesus as a result.

We both have fond memories of neighbors we had when we were growing up, who took a moment to show an interest and be available for a little conversation or a game of hangman, or who offered the chance to pick a handful of ripe cherries from their tree. Those few moments of interest let us know that we were cared for, and that someone besides our parents was looking out for us. Now we try to make sure we have a smile and an encouraging word for the kids in our neighborhood. And often, though they are unaware of it, we include them specifically in our prayers.

Many denominations in the world organize themselves and their ministry by parish, or geographical location, taking on responsibility for the physical and spiritual needs of a certain community. If we are not careful, we can tend to come home and "pull the drapes," rather than letting our homes and families serve as a lighthouse to our "parish," a neighborhood where some are living in the shadows of a dark world.

As we consider all parts of the vision for our families, we must ask ourselves, are we trying to escape our neighborhood or, by God's grace, are we willing to embrace it?

Focus

How well do we know our neighbors?

If they had a need, would they feel free to ask us for help?

Who on our block needs something right now?

List a prayer you could be praying now for each family on your block, or in your apartment building. Let your children help. Make it a point to pray for your neighbors on a regular basis.

Chapter Twenty-Two

Your Vision in Your World

When Jesus walked on the earth, general knowledge did not even include the fact that the planet is round. (We're sure *he* knew that, having made it and all, but no one else had figured it out yet.)

Today, thanks to technology, our globe is very, very small. This means that our family's reach is very, very long when it comes to spreading the news in every nation, as Jesus tells us to do in Mark 16:15 (TLB): "And then he told them, 'You are to go into all the world and preach the Good News to everyone, everywhere.'"

Our traditional ideas of participating in "foreign missions," as many churches refer to it, may limit our thinking. We may consider going on long- or short-term trips to other countries, or giving money to make it possible for others to do so, as the only options we have to participate. And while these choices are certainly necessary and effective options for families suited to such work, the assumption that they're the only ones is further from the truth today than ever before.

Few families who read this book will actually be called to serve on a foreign mission field, but all of us have contact daily with people from all corners of the globe, particularly if we have a presence on social media. Most responsible parents know the importance of teaching their children how to behave on social media, from taking precautions for safety to being careful about the messages they are sending about themselves in the photos and statuses they post. We work to develop hearts in our kids that would keep them from being cyberbullies, and we teach them to report such incidents when they become aware of them.

But you can be proactive in making social media a positive part of your family's life. Such places as Facebook, Instagram, and Twitter actually offer an option for your family vision to find effective outreach and to have impact on people in far-flung places. Just as missionaries on their way to Asia or South America must study the culture and learn the language in order to live and communicate effectively with those they are going to help, our families can study the culture of social media and discover ways to shine light there, as individuals or as a whole. It might even be that your family vision would be enhanced by blogging or developing a family website as a kind of outreach.

A great place to pursue our vision as it relates to the world is prayer. As children, we prayed something like "God bless Mother and Daddy and Brother and Sister and everybody else in the whole wide world. Amen." But we can make our family prayers much more specific and meaningful.

Begin by making it a practice to listen to a news broadcast, talk about the people involved in the events, both worldwide and locally, and think about the physical and spiritual needs they might have. Discussing current events with our kids, in light of Scripture, and then praying for individuals and nations involved takes away the instinct to react in fear or judgment, and it helps us develop sensitivity to those in need. It might be that our prayers alone are exactly what God is wanting from our family. If he is asking for more, it is through our prayers that we will become aware of his direction for us.

Obviously, we want to keep the level of information appropriate for the ages of our children. While teenagers could and should be aware, for example, of turmoil in the Middle East, even to the horrors of mass beheadings, elementary-aged children are not yet emotionally equipped to handle that level of information. However, little ones can grasp the need to pray for the family whose house has been destroyed by a fire, or pray for the mayor or the governor to make wise decisions.

The Internet also offers a great way for the family to become familiar with the world and the needs there. One of our favorite tools for this is Google Earth. If your church sponsors a missionary, try to get photos and biographical information for the family. Research the customs, the government, and the social and physical needs of the community where they are. Use Google Earth to zoom in on the village or town where they are placed. Sometimes you can even zoom in to the exact house where they live or the church or mission where they serve. This helps the family form concrete ideas of who and what they are praying for.

As your family begins to develop a connection, your kids can send encouraging emails to the missionary family and perhaps even send small gifts at birthdays and Christmas. Your family may discover some specific needs, not covered by the general mission association of your church, that you will find you can meet as a family project. Even the youngest members of the family can become engaged if we use the tools available to show them the world outside of their neighborhood.

Another way your family can use the Internet as a tool to discover how your vision can impact the world is to research nonprofit organizations that identify, and work to meet the needs of, communities or individuals in third-world countries. Children are orphaned, children are hungry, and children are in need of medical attention, and there are a number of reputable groups whose purpose is to make a way for concerned people to help meet those needs. Our family discovered an organization that does microfinancing for such communities and the individuals who live in them. The website is set up so that you can look through a list of needs and decide where you would like to invest your loan. Over the course of time, the person you have helped pays it back through the organization. When that is done, you get the opportunity to reinvest in someone else.

We have made it a tradition to invest in projects on behalf of family members at Christmastime. Over the past few years, gifts that we have given our kids, or received from them, have included a goat for a family that needed the milk both to feed themselves and to sell. We also bought candy for a single mother to stock a store she operated out of her house through microfinancing loans at kiva.org. And we donated funds to dig a well for a village that needed a source of clean water. It has become a favorite part of our holiday celebration, which includes prayers specifically for the people on the other side of the world who will benefit from our investments.

We know a couple who were already grandparents when they went with a handful of others just across the border from Texas into Mexico to visit an orphanage on a day trip that was organized as a one-time project by their church. Their hearts were captured by the children there, and they began to make regular trips on their own in order to deliver items they had gathered, from new underwear for all the kids to toys and treats.

One Saturday, they took their teenaged granddaughter with them. In playing with the children and talking to them, she discovered that it was one little boy's birthday. On the trip home, she told her grandparents that she wanted to go back once a month and throw a birthday party for the kids who had birthdays that month. Thrilled to have a project to work on with their granddaughter, and especially one that included their newfound passion for the children in that orphanage, they agreed to help her. Each month, they would head to Mexico with birthday gifts and party decorations, in addition to the other items they had gathered. They would stop, once they had crossed the border, and buy pizza, soda, and birthday cake, and then host a great party for the kids.

Their children and other grandchildren were intrigued by the photos and stories they brought back each month, and before a year had passed, the entire family was involved. When they discovered a makeshift camp of homeless families living far from town, they began to deliver large quantities of rice and beans and other necessities on every trip as well. Now, three generations of just one family work together every month to substantially meet the needs of both the orphans and the children living in poverty in that one little village, only a few hours' drive from their homes.

Whatever the vision that God has for how our family is to operate at home, as we look for ways to develop a passion for all people, we will find a way that we are able to bring Christ's love to the entire world.

YouTube Time Warp

One day, we were looking on the computer at video of little children in a South American village, and our grandson, who was then four years old, was nearby. He was drawn to the sounds of the children laughing, and he stood there, watching. As he looked, he noticed that they were not using a soccer ball, but a bag filled with trash. He asked us, "What is that they are kicking?"

When we explained that they could not afford a soccer ball, he immediately asked if we could buy one and send it to them. Touched by his little heartfelt desire to help, we helped him look online for a way to purchase and send soccer balls to such a village. Sure enough, we discovered just such an organization and opportunity online, and together with him, made the purchase and arranged for delivery, feeling excited about the lesson he had learned.

The next day, when he came to our house, he asked if he could see that video again, and glad to know that it had made such an impact, we quickly pulled it up and pressed play. As the children on the screen once again ran after the bag of trash, our grandson began to look surprised and then concerned.

"Hey!" he said. "Why aren't they using the new ball we got them?"

Focus

Where do we get our ideas and information about the rest of the world?

What places do we particularly connect with? Why?

As you hear the news each day, develop the habit of praying for the situations and the people involved in those stories. As a family, brainstorm ways to help.

Chapter Twenty-Three

Your Vision Becomes Your Reality

Setting out to identify God's vision for your family and then working to make it your daily reality may seem intimidating at this point.

But through Scripture, we find that God has specific instructions on how to make his vision part of who your family is. As a parent, you lead this project, so it is up to you to get the ball rolling. But the good news is that you don't have to do it by yourself. He has given us directions!

Here, then, is a list of specific Bible verses, along with a brief rehash of what we've talked about so far. Think of this as your list of "Six Hacks for Becoming a Family of Vision."

Seek God

"Seek the Kingdom of God above all else, and live righteously, and he will give you everything you need" (Matt. 6:33).

If God's vision for each family is unique, then we won't find that vision by randomly selecting an idea from some sort of menu.

"Hmm. Foreign missions. I love to travel. But wait. I hate mosquitoes. What's next on the list?"

No, the place to start is by prayerfully asking your Father to take your family—wherever you are and as you are today, as unconventional and quirky as that may seem to be—and begin to direct and guide and use you to his glory. As you talk together, as you read the Bible, and as you pray, you can trust that the ideas and insights that come to you are, indeed, his holy input.

And don't be surprised if what you discover is . . . a surprise!

Study Each Family Member Individually

"God's various gifts are handed out everywhere; but they all originate in God's Spirit. God's various ministries are carried out everywhere; but they all originate in God's Spirit. God's various expressions of power are in action everywhere; but God himself is behind it all. Each person is given something to do that shows who God is: Everyone gets in on it, everyone benefits. All kinds of things are handed out by the Spirit, and to all kinds of people! The variety is wonderful" (1 Cor. 12:4–6 *The Message*).

At some point as a new parent, the shocking realization dawns that your child is not your property, or an extension of your dreams. This little individual is really a tiny stranger, who from the beginning will have likes and preferences and little idiosyncrasies. From the time he was about eight weeks old, our youngest grandson would sometimes cry inconsolably for much longer than seemed healthy, for no reason apparent to his parents. During one of these episodes, Willie Nelson's "You Were Always On My Mind" came on the car radio, and in true Texas tradition, he immediately stopped crying, mid-wail, and settled right down. The next time the baby cried, our daughter, just to get a laugh from her husband, played it over her phone. To their surprise, the baby stopped crying right away. No one is sure why, but to this day, if the baby cries, Willie makes it right.

Recognizing that no two people of any age in your family are exactly alike in temperament, talents, or interests, it becomes important for parents to earnestly seek to know and understand each one. This is achieved by listening, purposefully observing, and initiating conversations where we ask more than we tell. And again, as we make it a point to pray for each individual in the family, asking God to help us see and understand that person as God has made him or her to be, we will find new and deeper insights begin to open for us.

As we discover more and more about the precious ones God has entrusted to our care, it will be important to express affirmation, approval, encouragement, and love to each separate member of the family, and to make it a point to consider and include them. In our family, dad is a musician and a sports fan, mom is a journalist who enjoys all forms of literature and loves the scenery of nature, our daughter loved plays and shows even as a child, and our son loves sports and history.

When we planned our family vacations, we tried to include activities that would hit on each person's interests over the course of the trip. So you would find us attending an outdoor musical, getting tickets to a baseball game, visiting a Revolutionary War museum, and taking in a photography exhibit at an art museum all as part of one vacation. And as we did those things, modeling interest in what was of interest to our loved ones, a fascinating thing happened. The girls actually became sports fans, and the guys began to really like attending Broadway musicals. Growing up, our daughter never missed one of her brother's games, and he never missed a performance that she was in. Even today, as adults, she is always pushing his yearbook sales, and he attends all of her department's plays, in addition to participating in and supporting each other in ministry.

So it's a key strategy to invest time, prayer, and effort into understanding what encourages and motivates each family member and into making sure each person knows that the rest of the family is behind him or her.

Assess Your Strengths and Weaknesses as a Group, and Work to Get It Right at Home

"Is there any encouragement from belonging to Christ? Any comfort from his love? Any fellowship together in the Spirit? Are your hearts tender and compassionate? Then make me truly happy by agreeing wholeheartedly with each other, loving one another, and working together with one mind and purpose. Don't be selfish; don't try to impress others. Be humble, thinking of others as better than yourselves. Don't look out only for your own interests, but take an interest in others, too" (Phil. 2:1–4).

So here you are, a perfectly lovely collection of individuals, created and gifted by God, and as the psalmist said, "set into a family." But, followers of Jesus though we all may be, if we are honest, we will admit that sharing the same address doesn't guarantee that there will be unity of purpose and spirit under that roof. In fact, we sometimes get into the habit of treating family members far worse than we would ever think of behaving toward friends or coworkers. So, once again, we have to hit our knees and ask God to give us insight into our family dynamic and the wisdom to improve the atmosphere in our home.

And the very first people who need to initiate those changes are mom and dad. It is a sometimes embarrassing fact that our children merely reflect what we are showing them from day to day. Consideration, courtesy, and respect should be the norm in all of our interactions with one another. When things get scratchy and the pressure is on, instead of indulging those flashes of emotion and reacting to them, we have to teach ourselves to exercise self-control and prayerfully choose to respond instead.

Learning to model charity, mercy, and grace toward one another in the privacy of our homes will lend authenticity to what people outside our family observe about us.

Find Out What Your Family Is Good At

"Be generous with the different things God gave you, passing them around so all get in on it: if words, let it be God's words; if help, let it be God's hearty help. That way, God's bright presence will be evident in everything through Jesus, and *he'll* get all the credit as the One mighty in everything—encores to the end of time" (1 Pet. 4:8–11 *The Message*).

Now it's time to look at the fam as a whole and figure out what it is that you do best together. We've talked about families whose thing was music, or football, or foreign missions. We've looked at folks who were groundskeepers, who foster special-needs children, or who build houses in Mexico. We've seen families whose gifting was for hospitality, and others with a broad list of different endeavors.

So what are the things that you get a great sense of unity, and pleasure, out of doing together? When you do those things, is there an important role that each family member fulfills? If nothing comes immediately to mind, then maybe you could get your feet wet by trying out different areas of service and gauging your effectiveness and fulfillment level as a family there. Volunteer one night at a homeless shelter, or operate the church nursery one Wednesday night on a trial basis.

Is there a need that you see, in the church or in your community, that you could begin to meet somehow by using those skills and interests? Is there a place that you could undertake such a project, even on a small scale, right now? Is there anything that would keep you from being able to do that? What could you do to overcome any perceived obstacles?

The crucial question is where you are and what your family is involved in right now. Where have you established relationships and a circle of influence? What is it you do that allows every member of the family to participate and even to shine? Or maybe the question is, what is the hardest thing your family has had to overcome? Are there others struggling with that same thing, who could use your understanding and support? Is that something God could use you in?

Once again, it's time to pray like a detective. Ask God to uncover ideas and opportunities that you may have been unaware of. Ask him to reveal his plans and his purposes in putting you all together. You can be certain that if you ask, he will show you what he desires your family to be and do.

Look for a Place to Help

"So no matter what your task is, work hard. Always do your best as the Lord's servant, not as man's, because you know your reward is the Lord's inheritance. You serve the Lord, the Anointed One" (Col. 3:23–24 *The Voice*).

Now you are ready to find a place for your family to practice living out your vision.

Your family's desire to help the homeless people in your city probably won't be fulfilled by opening a shelter next month. But your family certainly is needed in your church's outreach, or at one of the shelters already operating in your town.

Remembering that God's vision for your family is always practical, and it starts with your family as you are, look for the places where you could contribute. It is likely that you have already noticed a need, that your hearts already have been drawn to something, even if up until now it was just the thought that "someone should . . ."

But if not, hop onto the good old Internet and Google around. If your church doesn't have something specific to your ideas, chances are good that there is a nonprofit charitable organization that does. Could they use your family as volunteers? Or maybe it's just a matter of gassing up the lawn mower and setting out in search of a place where the weeds are winning and people would welcome your help.

And finally, if this is beginning to sound like a repetitious theme, that's because it is: pray! Ask God to show you when, where, and how you can apply his vision to your family life.

Do Something

"*Act* on what you hear! Those who hear and don't act are like those who glance in the mirror, walk away, and two minutes later have no idea who they are, what they look like" (James 1:22–23 *The Message*).

Did you ever have stage fright? Ever climb to the top of the high dive at a public pool, and then have to weigh whether it will be worse to somehow die from the dive or suffer the humiliation of having to push past the ones behind you and climb back down? What if your first, or tenth, or sixtieth attempt at living out your vision flops? What if someone in your family makes a tragic choice that makes you all look bad?

So what? The results of mission and ministry are not your responsibility. Nope. *God* is responsible for the outcome of our efforts, all the time, every time. It may be that we never in this life have even a glimpse of the outcome of our efforts to serve and honor him. The Maker of the universe has lovingly crafted each member of your family, and he has graciously granted you the vision he has for your joy and fulfillment and your usefulness in his kingdom.

Whatever it is that your family is designed to do, don't let another week pass without putting your vision into action! That first effort is always the hardest, because you are covering new territory, but anyone who has ever timidly carried a tray into the cafeteria on the first day of school knows that within a week, lunch period will be old hat.

So now it's time to get started. Picture that infamous swoosh embossed on your roof, and just . . . do it! Your family, and your world, will be eternally glad you did.

Clarify Your Vision on a Family Weekend Retreat

If you are motivated and ready to actively become a family of vision, a great first official step would be to plan a weekend family retreat for that express purpose.

One weekend out of fifty-two is not a big investment for the return that your family will receive from an annual family retreat. This is your opportunity to combine creativity and purpose, with the result being clarity in your family's vision. Don't expect it to be another of the fun getaways that you all enjoy at other times of the year, even though this should be far from a solemn occasion. A family retreat has a bigger purpose that reaches beyond a good time and relaxation.

At your first family retreat, your goal will be to come away with a picture of what your family's vision is. You'll use a lot of the guidance that you find in this book to achieve that. In all the retreats that follow, your purpose will be to review and refresh that vision. Discovering new interests or talents, finding yourself in new circumstances and situations, or identifying new opportunities might cause you to tweak or expand your vision.

To ensure that your family is successful, an outline follows of what should be included.

Prepare and Plan

As much as any other important event in your family life, the retreat weekend needs to be well planned. Find a place with few distractions and no overhyped attractions nearby, trying their very best to lure your kids in. And maybe you, too.

Depending on how outdoorsy your family is, your accommodations might be anything from a campsite to a hotel room. It doesn't need to be far from home, but far enough that the setting will not be familiar to the point of being ho-hum.

Put together a fairly tight schedule for the weekend, making sure that every moment of your time is dedicated to your goal. Even every meal and every activity should reflect the weekend's theme. As far as possible, make meals a time where everyone participates in both cooking and cleanup, but keep it very simple and fast to do.

You're the one who sells this retreat idea to the whole family, so get excited about it!

Find Your Focus

Make the purpose of this weekend and how important it is well known throughout the entire family. Talk about it weeks in advance. As you prepare your schedule, look at each and every part of it and make sure that it enhances your focus and addresses what you want to accomplish. Keep in mind the ages and attention spans of each of your children and plan accordingly. Elementary age children can hang with you for about twenty minutes, and then they need a change. Teens should be good for forty-five minutes, but expecting them to stick with one activity for more than that is pushing it. So be purposeful in varying thinking, reading, writing, listening, movement, crafts, and so on.

Throughout the entire retreat, in each and every thing that happens, there are three key attributes that you want to build into the framework of your family's vision:

- Identity. Who are we as a family? What does it mean to be a part of our family? What things do we stand for?
- Involvement. What does our family do? What happens when we work together? How important is it that we support one another?
- Inclusion. What part does each of us play in building our family? How can we be sure that we always stand together? How can we each be different, but all of us a part of our family?

Make It Memorable

In case this is beginning to sound more like boot camp than a retreat, you need to know that this is the part where the good times come in. As important as it is to build your family vision during this time, you need to fill the weekend with the potential for great memories. If everyone isn't ready to do it again next year, then it's going to get more difficult to make it a success every time. The memorable times will also remind everyone of all the things you decided to become during the weekend. So make plenty of room for memorable moments throughout the retreat. Use your creativity and your imagination to come up with activities, games, and crafts that connect with what it means to be a family of vision.

The following seven quick retreat hacks might get your brain in motion:

- Create a family crest or coat of arms together. You can use art paper, crayons, magazine pictures, glue, glitter, scraps of fabric—whatever you gather up. As you work, talk about the meaning of the symbols on your coat of arms. You could even talk about the role of a shield in battle, and how that's what a family does for each other.
- Do a building project together that includes everyone's participation.

- Collect interesting things you find in nature and put together a foam-board collage.
- Make paper-bag puppets and write a play to perform as a family.
- Produce a "Family Awards Show" with special honors for each person in the family.
- Use a white plastic table cover and decorate it together.
- Put together a *huge* mobile with words that describe your family.
- Pray together for your family. One-sentence prayers around the circle are something that anyone can take part in.
- If you're still at a loss for things to do, Google "family activities" or "family fun," or go to parents.com and search there.

Everybody Owns It

Make sure everyone understands that this is not going to be a time where rules and regulations are laid out but a discussion about who your family is and how God might want to use you all together.

The weekend will be open to everyone's thoughts, input, opinions, and ideas. As you do more of these weekends and your kids get older, they can take an active role in planning and presenting for these retreats. Remember that, even with this wide-open conversation, you're still the one who has the responsibility to make certain everyone is kind and positive, and that each person has the opportunity to participate.

You'll find that these retreats will become something you can point to as being life-changing in your family. Learn from it, and begin to live out your vision as a family every day.

Focus

What is one thing we can do this week to get started on becoming a family of vision?

Chapter Twenty-Four

Shaped by Your Vision

God's vision for your family starts exactly where you are today, and it takes you where you are going. But, like the pillar of fire and the manna in the wilderness, God's leading is day by day on the journey.

Whenever we speak about finding God's vision for the family, we usually end by simply telling our story. We've noticed that, as we do, people's faces lighten up, and they begin to smile, like they're thinking, "Oh, we *can* do this!" So we want to end our book by inviting you to sit in on a conversation, as we talk about our own family vision and how it has unfolded over thirty-plus years.

Martha: When we met, Greg was the youth pastor at our church, and I was a high school teacher, new to San Antonio, who volunteered to teach a high school Sunday school class. Although we might not have fully realized it at that time, our separate visions for loving and investing in young people were one of the things we had in common, that drew us to each other.

We both really liked teenagers, and we wanted to make things fun for them. More importantly, we wanted to do what we could to help them successfully navigate the decisions and pressures of that time in their lives. We realized then that what home is like has a huge impact on the kind of person a child grows up to be.

Greg: As we began married life together, we chose to make Proverbs 3:5 a key verse to guide us in our lives. *The Message* puts it this way: "Trust GOD from the bottom of your heart; don't try to figure out everything on your own. Listen for GOD's voice in everything you do, everywhere you go; he's the one who will keep you on track."

We tried to live this out, consciously choosing to make our day-to-day living line up with this principle. Don't get me wrong. We missed the boat a few times and made plenty of messes along the way. That perfect family we discussed back in Chapter Four is definitely not us!

But God did do his part to keep us on track in spite of ourselves.

Martha: As parents, we knew it was important to guide our children toward their own personal relationships with Jesus, so we invested a lot of time and effort into making him the center of activities and conversations at home, and we included the kids in prayer times and service projects, and we took them with us to youth group events and camps and on school trips to journalism workshops all over the country. We got really good at folding the Pack 'n Play and probably should have invested in stock for Wet Wipes. It was a great day for us when they were finally old enough to pack their own suitcases! But because they were always a part of what we were doing, they grew up thinking that our work and our ministry was a family operation.

Greg: Although my specific occupations varied over the years, from pastoring to sports media and marketing to various entrepreneurial endeavors, our focus was always on how we could serve God in any situation, and of course Martha, as a public-school teacher, had lots of opportunity to offer his love and model redemption to many teens. Because they were around a lot, and because of our breakfast and dinner conversations, our own kids picked up on that idea.

Martha: And, probably because offering love and encouragement to others was important to us, we were always talking to our kids about how they could be doing that at school, starting in elementary school and carrying through their high school years. As they progressed through public school, our kids began to notice that not all of their friends had a peaceful family life, and some were dealing with heavy problems. They would come home and tell us about things their friends were going through, and we would pray for them. In those early years, our prayers included everything from a dad who was deployed to Iraq, to a mom who had cancer, to the loss of a pet. As the kids got older, they also began to question how they could help.

Greg: One year, when the kids were in upper elementary and middle school, I decided that we should have a family retreat, and instead of spending time playing board games and fishing or tossing a football around, as we usually would do on getaway weekends, we would spend the time in prayer and Bible study, asking God to give us a vision for what he wanted us to focus on as a family during the coming year.

I had wondered to myself if the kids would be able to stay focused for that long, but they were totally engaged the entire time. We came away with such a sense of unity and direction that we made the family retreat a yearly event. As the kids grew older, we gave them responsibility for directing parts of the weekend, and we were always amazed at the maturity and depth of what they would contribute.

Martha: I will never forget the year that Annie came with visual aids and activities for her part, or the year that Matt had a chart with his five points, all alliteratively beginning with the letter *P*. We probably should have known then the directions they were headed!

Greg: Meanwhile, outside of our home life and careers, Martha and I were busy teaching classes for teens, college and career students, young married couples, and then for parents in general, whenever we were asked by our pastor to do so. Out of those engagements came invitations to lead family workshops and seminars, and in an attempt to make the presentations fun and engaging, we often made up skits, including our kids as characters in our imaginary family scenarios. As we were preparing those skits, our kids enthusiastically contributed ideas, so the final presentation was truly a family production.

Martha: Again, in retrospect, Matt introduced comedy, and Annie was great at developing characters and knowing how to arrange the set and use props. They each added so much to what we were doing, but at the time I didn't think much about how these experiences would feed into who they would be as adults. I just knew that doing these things as a family, with everyone contributing, was a source of joy and fulfillment for all of us.

Martha: Another project that involved the whole family every year was making our front-yard Christmas display. We began in October, brainstorming ideas for a cool display that would point toward the wonderful news that God is with us. Once we settled on a theme, we would spend lots of Saturdays and weeknights out in the garage, using the jigsaw and painting and creating extra touches. As December 1 got closer, lights had to be strung and music recorded on a loop. There's a reason we refer to ourselves as the Griswolds!

Greg: Yeah, anyone remember the movie *Christmas Vacation*? We lived it! But the great thing was that we were all aware that this was a gift we were giving to our neighbors. Our subdivision was serious about its lighting and decoration contest, so we had lots of traffic passing by all month, including many of Martha's students and the kids' school friends. The process was lots of fun for our family, but the idea of pointing others to Jesus as a family was always there.

Martha: I love to cook, and we always enjoyed inviting friends and family to our house for a meal. As our kids became teens, it was only natural that they would ask friends over, too. Remembering our days as youth pastors, we often made our house available for youth group parties and sleepovers.

Greg: But something deeper was happening as we sat around the table. Conversations would turn to where people were in life. Sometimes we would be celebrating blessings that our friends encountered, or we would be talking about seeking God's direction as seasons changed for our guests. And sometimes, there would be an honest sharing of hurts and fears and disappointments, and we would be able to pray and encourage our friends. Our kids were always a part of this interaction.

Martha: As we had prayerfully decided that our kids should both attend the inner-city high school where I was teaching, wanting them to understand that not everyone enjoyed the same blessings in life they had, an interesting thing began to happen. Our kids began to bring their school friends home. A lot! And I have to tell you that this is where the Lord and I had to have some serious conversations about just how important clean bathrooms and soda spilled on carpet really were in the eternal scheme of things. It turns out that in my case, the answer was . . . not very.

Greg: The kids were both very active at school. Annie was into theater, choir, and yearbook, and she was a member of several campus clubs. Matt played football, led Fellowship of Christian Athletes, and was on yearbook staff, too. They both knew lots of people and felt free to invite friends over on an almost daily basis. We were always glad to welcome them, and Martha always had a freezer full of pizza and taquitos, a truckload of chips, and lots of soda on hand.

Martha: But the interesting thing is that our kids began to bring home with them the ones that were hurting, or struggling, as well. These kids would end up at our dinner table, where encouragement and wise counsel and just plain old love and acceptance could be a natural part of the conversation. The fact that I also taught many of their friends was not without its moments, though. I will never forget opening the door one Saturday afternoon, early in the school year, to find one of my new students who had dropped by to see Annie. "Hey, come on in!" I greeted him, stepping back to motion him inside. Halfway in the door, he threw on the brakes, eyes wide and mouth hanging open. "Mrs. Sing!" he exclaimed. "You're not wearing *shoes*!"

Martha: We attended all of the games, the plays, the concerts, and other events at the high school. Between me hosting yearbook and newspaper staff parties, and Annie hosting cast parties after plays and concerts, there were a lot of kids through our house. We were always glad to have the kids over after dances, and we hosted an all-night food and games extravaganza after prom. After football games, it got to be a habit Annie's senior year for most of the players to show up at our house, which seemed a little unusual week after week. I thought maybe it was because, in addition to hanging with Annie and her friends, who were always fun to be around, I always had lots of food and there was never alcohol that could get them into trouble with the coach. Then one week I noticed that when the guys came in, they would greet Annie and me, and then ask, "Where's Mr. Sing?" And it dawned on me that these were boys who didn't have dads at home, or whose parents didn't attend their games. They were there for the attention and affirmation Greg would give them as they rehashed each play, and each boy's role in it.

Greg: Annie graduated and left for college, but as Matt continued to play football, his teammates continued to hang out at our house. We never knew on a Saturday morning who would be sleeping on our living room floor when we got up. Sometimes, picking our way over all the bodies to get to the coffeepot was a physical challenge, because in Texas, offensive linemen in high school are *big*! While that meant an increase in our food budget during those years, it was lots of fun for us, and we always counted it a privilege to get to love those kids.

Martha: And it was always humbling to know that when we hugged them good-bye, and told them that we loved them or were proud of them, it might be the only hug or expression of affirmation they got all week. We knew that God had brought us to that place and time in our family's life for his purpose.

Greg: So, because of the things they had experienced, and after seeking God's leading and direction for their own futures, our children headed off to college. Annie went to Oral Roberts University to earn a degree in theatre arts education. While there, she met her future husband, a youth ministry major. Matt earned both a bachelor's and a master's degree in education from Baylor University.

They each left home with a desire to return and teach at the same high school as Martha, because they had developed such a love for the community and a burden for the specific needs there.

Martha: Today, you will find Annie teaching drama and Matt teaching journalism there. Matt also pastors a home church designed with people from his old group of friends in mind, and the church has adopted the school community as the focus of their service projects and general care. In his job as youth pastor, our son-in-law was in charge of camps and retreats. It always seemed like a no-brainer that I would cook for camp, Greg would direct the games, and Matt would act as a counselor and teach break-out sessions, because working together in ministry was just what we did. Now that they are part of the small home church that Matt pastors, Annie and her husband meet with students from the school once a week at a nearby restaurant, where the church buys the kids tacos, and Annie and Robbie are available to talk with them on any subject, or to lead Bible study to help the kids find answers to their questions.

For the most part, these are not kids who have grown up attending church, so they were really excited when the members of the house church decided to fund a retreat for them. They got to hike and fish and play "sardines," new experiences for most of them. And then, on the last morning, five of them asked Robbie if he would baptize them in the river.

Greg: Matt's church meets at our house on Sunday nights. Martha cooks dinner for everyone, and after we eat together, we move to the living room for sharing and Bible study. So our house is still full of people, and our dinner table is still a place for sharing.

Martha: A really neat thing happened a couple of months ago. One of Matt's friends, who spent a lot of time here when he was in high school and college, dropped by to see us. While his home life growing up was hectic and unstable, he worked his way through college and is now the father of three, and has a great job. As we visited and exclaimed over photos of his kids, he looked at Greg and said, "I just want you to know that I wouldn't have any idea how to be a dad, if it weren't for all the time I spent here with you guys. I just want to say thank you."

Greg: So that's the story of how God's vision for our family has unfolded over the years . . . so far. It was the natural outgrowth of God taking us as who we are and where we are, and using our willingness to follow and serve him to weave us together for his purposes, day by day and year by year.

Martha: It was really so simple, and it has been so sweet. And the exciting thing is that he's not through with us, either. His vision for us going forward will still start with where we are today and take us where we are going!

We would be delighted to assist you in any way possible as you begin to seek and live out God's vision for your own family, or just to hear the story of how your vision develops. Always feel free to contact us via our website: www.marthaandgregsingleton.com.

We pray for God's richest blessings on you and every member of you family now and for generations to come!

Notes

Chapter Two

[1]tasser10, "A Scrapbook of Rick Neuheisel's Great UCLA Moments," *Bruins Nation* (blog), December 15, 2011, http://www.bruinsnation.com/2011/12/15/2638403/a-scrapbook-of-rick-neuheisels-great-ucla-moments.

Chapter Three

[1]Don Pierson, "Singletary Still Leaves Impression," *Chicago Tribune*, July 30, 1998, http://articles.chicagotribune.com/1998-07-30/sports/9807300098_1_leslie-frazier-paul-krause-gary-fencik.

Chapter Seven

[1]Tertullian, "Chapter 39," *Apology*, trans. S. Thelwall, http://www.logoslibrary.org/tertullian/apology/39.html.

Chapter Nine

[1]Mama Sass, "What's Wrong with Today's Teenagers?," *Miami Herald*, February 25, 2014, http://www.miamiherald.com/latest-news/article1960746.html.

[2]J. Ronald Oakley, *God's Country: America in the Fifties* (New York: W.W. Norton, 1986). Available online at www.colorado.edu/AmStudies/lewis/1025/godscountry.pdf.

[3]H. M., "Letter to the Chicago Tribune," *Chicago Tribune*, May 20, 1928, republished at http://americainclass.org/sources/becomingmodern/modernity/text1/colcommentarymodernyouth.pdf.

[4]Attributed to Socrates by Plato, according to William L. Patty and Louise S. Johnson, *Personality and Adjustment* (Columbus, OH: McGraw-Hill, 1953), 277.

[5]Elaine Reese, "What Kids Learn from Hearing Family Stories," *Atlantic*, December 9, 2013, www.theatlantic.com/education/archive/2013/12/what-kids-learn-from-hearing-family-stories/282075/.

Chapter Ten

[1]Mark Kelly, "LifeWay Research Looks at Role of Faith in Parenting," LifeWay, March 24, 2009, www.lifeway.com/Article/LifeWay-Research-looks-at-role-of-faith-in-parenting.

Chapter Eleven

[1]Fred Rogers, *The World According to Mister Rogers: Important Things to Remember* (New York: Hachette Books, 2003), 162.

[2]ESPN, *The Book of Manning*, ESPN Films/Front Row Films, 2013, https://vimeo.com/132339059.

Chapter Fifteen

[1]Jennifer R. Lloyd, "Elf Louise to distribute 55,000 presents to needy kids," *San Antonio Express-News,* November 25, 2013, http://www.mysanantonio.com/san_antonio_charity/article/Elf-Louise-to-distribute-55-000-presents-to-needy-5001478.php.

Chapter Sixteen

[1]WLIB, "The Winans Brothers talk about new album 'Foreign' and being on a reality show," WLIB radio interview, November 14, 2014, https://www.youtube.com/watch?v=KooBrznA-4c.

[2]Richard Harrington, "First Family of Gospel," *Washington Post,* April 5, 1992, https://www.washingtonpost.com/archive/lifestyle/style/1992/04/05/first-family-of-gospel/6e38d0f6-195e-4e22-8c73-459be6b024a8/.

[3]Elizabeth Atkins, "Delores Winans on Marriage, Faith and Family," *BLAC Detroit,* May 2013, www.blacdetroit.com/BLAC-Detroit/May-2013/Delores-Winans-on-Marriage-Faith-and-Family.

About the Authors

Faith and family are the passions that drive what Martha and Greg Singleton do.

Over the years, Greg worked at varied careers, ranging from pastoring a church, being on staff as both music and youth director, and serving as media information director for a USFL football team, to marketing and public relations. Greg is currently president of NextBigStep, Inc., a nonprofit organization dedicated to providing counsel, encouragement, and inspiration for those transitioning into new life situations.

Chosen as one of the Top Ten Teachers in Texas by the University of Texas, Martha was also named by the Dow Jones Newspaper Fund and the Wall Street Journal as one of four Distinguished Newspaper Advisers in America in 2007. In her career as a high school journalism teacher, Martha built some of the nation's most highly acclaimed scholastic journalism programs. Martha recently retired from the classroom to dedicate more time to writing and speaking with Greg.

Meanwhile, the Singletons have been featured speakers at family and parenting conferences, seminars, workshops, schools, churches, organizations, and businesses across the country, sharing their insights with pragmatism and humor for groups as varied as the Billy Graham Evangelistic Association and the Texas Education Agency. They have appeared on numerous radio, television, and online broadcasts, including being featured in a two-part series on *FamilyLife Today*, hosted by Dr. Dennis Rainey and heard on over nine hundred radio stations around the world. Their unique abilities as communicators have brought insight and strategies to families across the country.

Perhaps the most significant validations of Greg and Martha's ministry to families are the resumes of their own children. Anne is a graduate of Oral Roberts University, with a degree in education. She teaches high school theatre arts in San Antonio, Texas. Anne is married to Robbie Bridges, who has served church staffs as a youth pastor and children's pastor, and is currently a manager with a Fortune 100 financial institution. Together, they take an active role in working with teens in the community. Anne and Robbie are the parents of eight-year-old Josiah and two-year-old Levi, Greg and Martha's grandsons. The Singletons' son, Matt, holds a BS and an MS in education from Baylor University. While he attended Baylor, he was also on the pastoral staff at University Baptist Church in Waco, Texas. He teaches high school journalism and also pastors a house church in San Antonio.

"From the beginning, we determined to build our home and relationship on biblical principles, striving to make them real and relevant through the days, weeks, and years," Martha said, "and our children, by God's grace, have chosen to join us in the journey."

The Singletons invite you to visit their website at www.marthaandgregsingleton.com, where you can find information about their podcasts, or contact them. They would like to hear from you.